# The Adventures of a Blind and Disabled Award-Winning Author

## Inspiration & Motivation to Empower You to Go for Your Own Gold Medals

### Shirley Cheng

www.DanceWithYourHeart.com

**Wappingers Falls, New York**

Copyright © 2009 by Shirley Cheng

ISBN: 978-0-6151-7515-7
Library of Congress Control Number: 2008901023

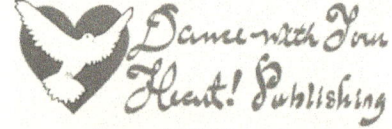

www.DanceWithYourHeart.com
Wappingers Falls, New York, United States of America

Star Rays Front Cover Background:
© Roberto Giovannini | Dreamstime.com

Some of the names in this memoir have been changed to protect the individuals' privacy.

All rights reserved by the author, Shirley Cheng. No part of this publication may be reproduced, stored in a retrieval system, or transmitted in any form or by any means, electronic, mechanical, photocopying, recording or otherwise, without the prior written permission of Shirley Cheng.

To my beloved mother Juliet Cheng, I dedicate this book. She is my supporter, my companion, my sidekick as we enjoy adventures together. No adventure can ever be fun, exciting, safe or promising without her. Thank you, Mom, for bringing me into this world so we can have a blast together!

# Table of Contents

Preface ..................................................................... 7
Prologue ................................................................... 9
Chapter I: The Life of an Author Begins ............................. 13
Chapter II: Fruits of Positivity, Passion, Purpose ................. 17
Chapter III: Sweet-Bearing Pain ........................................ 26
Are You Unstoppable? .................................................. 37
Chapter IV: Be the Star You Are! ..................................... 44
Chapter V: Hunting for Dr. Right ..................................... 48
Chapter VI: The Tough Getting Tougher .............................. 54
Chapter VII: Good Luck Year of the Dog ............................ 59
Dance with Your Heart .................................................. 66
Chapter VIII: Spreading the Inspiration ............................. 71
Celebrate Your Existence, for It Is Your Privilege! ............... 79
Chapter IX: Prevailing Maternal Love ............................... 83
Chapter X: Taking the Great with the Okay ......................... 88
Chapter XI: Twice a Winner ............................................ 93
Chapter XII: Remembering the Courage of a Lioness ............. 99
Chapter XIII: Seizing Opportunities, Taking Chances ............ 109
Chapter XIV: Flying with Faith ....................................... 114
Chapter XV: Pushing Forward .......................................... 120
Chapter XVI: Wheeling on the Red Carpet .......................... 131
Chapter XVII: Never an Ending, Always a Beginning ............. 137

Spirituality: the Secret to Everlasting Success .................... 142

Chapter XVIII: More Adventures in the Big Apple ........... 148

Chapter XIX: Appreciating the Purity of Life .................... 155

Chapter XX: NYC, Home of Adventures ........................... 163

Chapter XXI: Pushing Onward Still ................................... 169

Spotlight Raves ................................................................. 183

About the Author .............................................................. 192

# *Preface*

Where in life has the most doors from which to choose? The place is life itself. As we journey down our paths, we run into countless doors; each will take us to a different road, changing our life in one way or another, and it is up to us to pick which door to open, while hoping what lies behind will lead us to a golden valley, not a monster that will jump out to eat us up. Once opened, we cannot close the door again, so whatever we may face, we will simply have to do our best with what we have got.

Yet there are doors that life opens for us, doors that we cannot help but enter—unknowingly. Therefore, with every step we take, we must brace for whatever lies ahead, and do our utmost to choose doors that may positively impact the roads to which we are brought. I have run into both kinds of doors, and this book tells my journey and how I have spent my travel.

My story herein begins with one particular door that drastically affected my life: it veiled my eyes. Many would find that to be a horrible outcome, and although I would not call it as such, I would not say that it is a thrill, yet it itself did bring me much thrills. What has been done cannot be undone, and it was up to me to make the best of my situation.

Life took away my eyesight, I brought forth a new vision. In the following pages, you will explore my new vision and travel along with my beloved mother Juliet Cheng and me on our paths, exploring the brave new world to which the loss of my eyesight has led us. You will read many of my firsts—my first book signing, my first radio interview, my first trip to Las Vegas—and together, we will rediscover what thrills, delights, and challenges these firsts have brought my mother and me.

Thus, let us return to the wondrous roads, roads I would not have otherwise traveled, and in turn, relished, if I had not lost my eyesight.

# *Prologue*

Her small hands flew about the keyboard as a word appeared on the laptop screen every second, yet only her two index fingers touched the keys. A smile played at her lips as she envisioned the words on the screen and the images in her heart, which gently tells her all that it saw. Meanwhile her computer read aloud each key she typed. Her talking computer was a good companion; it never got tired of reading to her, unlike a person, who would periodically need to take a breath. No matter how long her computer had been reading, it would never fail to continue, with just a single down-arrow command from her. From the exciting to the boring, from the poems to the gripping autobiography she wrote, it read. Yet unlike a person, it could not read the graphic text, such as the verification codes found on many Web sites, so she had to ask her mother to read them to her.

On this day, she listened to what her computer said, more intensively than usual. Her heart pounded as she arrowed down the list of winners and Honorable Mentions. She was on the DIY (Do It Yourself) Web site, where the results of the 2007 DIY Book Festival were posted. She inwardly crossed her fingers as she went down the first list for the poetry category, in which she had entered her book. Would she win?

No, she was not a first-place winner. Maybe, just maybe —

Her mother in the next room heard a small but long squeal. "What is it, Pearl?"

"Mom, I received an Honorable Mention!" She could not believe her ears. She had to listen to it again. She pressed the up arrow so her computer could read the previous line.

*"Waking Spirit - Prose & Poems the Spirit Sings - Shirley Cheng,"* it promptly read.

"Yes, I got an Honorable Mention!" Shirley squealed again. Her book was the last one listed in the poetry category, so it came to her as a complete surprise. "Again!"

Her mother stopped whatever she was doing in the adjoining room and rushed out. "I'm so thrilled!" She laughed. "When I heard you squealing like that, I knew you must have some news. Another Honorable Mention! That is super." No, it was more than super, but what word in the human language could describe such happiness?

"Now I must write the press release," Shirley said to herself more than to her mother. Every time she had anything news worthy to share with the world, whether it be a new book release, a contest won, or an upcoming engagement, she would write the press release and post it on her blog, submit it to free press release sites, and E-mail it to the local media. She would also send out an announcement to her E-newsletter, *Shirley's Book News,* which she had started when her first book was in production. But the first place on which she would make her news available was her Web site, www.shirleycheng.com, which she had designed and maintained on her own. She remembered the basic HTML codes from when she was sixteen, when she had created eighty-six Web sites.

In a matter of minutes, Shirley finished writing the release; she had to write only the news portion, because she kept everything else, including her short biography, the same for most of her releases.

The 2007 DIY Book Festival awarded the title of Honorable Mention to *Waking Spirit: Prose & Poems the Spirit Sings* by Shirley Cheng, her third accolade for this book.

"What can I possibly say this time?" says Cheng, a blind and physically disabled 24-year-old author and motivational speaker. "Last time, I said I was floating on Cloud Nine. Well, let's say I'm dancing on it now."

*Waking Spirit*'s last two accolades were an Award-Winning Finalist in the national Indie Excellence 2007 Book Awards and an Honorable Mention in the 2007 New York Book Festival.

Shirley leaned back, even though she had nothing to lean against. She was on her bed; the cozy bedroom was her favorite place to be, and it was just the spot where she could write with peace and quiet. October 21, 2007. The date would be etched in the memory book deep in her heart for as long as her soul was in existence. She sighed contentedly. She was pleased with her progress. Her career as an author had brought her many surprises and happy memories. She thought back to how it all began and had to smile. She had been telling people, "Since I no longer could express myself in my artwork (I was an artist of the visual arts), I turned to writing to share with others my imagined worlds and creations." Although that was absolutely true, it was much simpler. She became an author because she lost her eyesight. It was as plain and simple as that.

Never had she imagined that she would become an author. But then, never had she imagined that she would lose her eyesight. Life indeed does bring many surprises, and she welcomed all, both good and bad, and had done her best dealing with the many challenges being a blind writer had brought her way.

She had certainly come a long way. She still remember the feel of the newly printed book in her hands, and how thrilled she was to hold a book; but it was not just any book—it was her book, with her creations, with her magical world...

# Chapter 9
# The Life of an Author Begins

Shirley ran her index finger down the length of the spine, enjoying its cool sensation. She flipped through the book, at first taking each page between her fingers to feel its crispness. In her mind's eye, she pictured the words against the off-white paper. The batch of her books had just arrived; the good batch. Being a blind writer, she had missed quite a few typographical errors in the first few proof copies she received via E-mail, and had had to send several corrections to her publisher until she was unable to find any more errors. That did not mean that there were no more errors left. Even though she listened carefully to every word the computer read, it was hard, for example, to catch words that were missing the S in the end. She had done her best and had put her heart and soul into writing the book she held in her hands. She had always enjoyed feeling books in her hands, but no feeling could ever match the wondrous feeling of holding her own book. The newest batch arrived months after her book's initial November 2003 publication, in time for her first book signing on February 19, 2005.

Not only had she encountered difficulty catching her own typographical errors, but she also faced the same problem catching the ones her publisher made. In actuality, her mother had missed the errors. The publisher had sent her the cover files, but since her computer could not read text on images, her mother had had to look them over. As a result, with the final batch, a typographical error graced its title on the front cover: *Daring Quest of Mystics*, which was supposed to be *Daring Quests of Mystics*.

She was very much looking forward to signing all three of her books, two of which she would be self-publishing and releasing before February. She wanted to self-publish her first book, but the laptop, which her school had loaned her, did not have Microsoft Word, so she was unable to format her manuscript. Lulu, the printer she would use, required that all manuscripts be formatted ready to print. Lulu is a company that provides the publishing tools for self-publishers and allows them to retain the full copyright and control of their work. Her grandmother Kwi Show would order a new laptop for her from a local computer store, and the president of the store would personally set it up and install the screen-reading software JAWS at her home. She could hardly wait to be her own boss. She knew that there would be plenty of work involved, but she was one who thoroughly enjoyed staying busy and figuring out things on her own. She often hungered for a good challenge, and publishing her own books without eyesight would no doubt hold many challenges. She craved them.

It would be her first time using Microsoft Word with JAWS, so she would have to figure out its techniques and features; that would be the first step in publishing. She would layout her manuscripts as she went along. Next, she would have to convert the formatted manuscripts into pdf files. She performed a search on the Internet and installed two free pdf converters, both of which she tried but only one was compatible with JAWS—that was all she needed.

It was about time that she set her other two books free to the world. She had written the books last year at age twenty, recently finishing the third, *Dance with Your Heart: Tales and Poems That the Heart Tells*, which had just been professionally edited.

When Shirley received her new laptop with everything properly set up and installed, she immediately set to work. It had the newest version of JAWS, version 5.0, so she first had to figure out how to use some of its many new features. She had figured out the previous JAWS version, 4.02, the first and only version she had been using, mostly on her own, so she was confident that she would not encounter difficulty with the new version. As she had expected, she was using JAWS 5.0 like a pro shortly thereafter, and had little problem using Microsoft Word. She was delighted that JAWS 5.0 worked much better; unlike the prior version, it did not freeze often when she worked with long manuscripts. Before, she had had a hard time working with her 185,000-word autobiography, *The Revelation of a Star's Endless Shine*, which caused JAWS and the entire laptop to freeze. Sometimes, she had to restart the laptop, often resulting in lost work. JAWS uses up a lot of virtual memory, slowing the functionality of any open programs, so she still had to restart her computer after she had worked on a large file for a few hours.

When December arrived, Shirley officially released *Dance with Your Heart*. She had hoped that she could release her autobiography, but Lulu had experienced a glitch, so she had to wait until January to publish it.

Being a new author, it was difficult spreading the word of her books. In addition, she was not simply a new author; she was a blind and physically disabled new author, making the task much harder. But then, it was the era of technology, and she could use the Internet to its fullest potential. She had subscribed to several E-newsletters targeting the publishing world, where she received valuable up-to-date information right in her inbox. In one newsletter, she read about a radio host, Maxine Thompson, who interviewed authors on her Internet radio show. Shirley immediately E-mailed her to see if she could be a future guest on her show. She was asked to mail in a copy of her book, so she sent out *Dance with Your Heart*, along with a media kit containing press releases and pertinent information about her books and her life. In mid-December, Shirley was thrilled to receive Maxine's E-mail inviting her on her show for January.

# Chapter 99
# Fruits of Positivity, Passion, Purpose

"I have a special guest tonight. Her name is Shirley Cheng," announced Maxine Thompson at the start of the interview on January 19. "And she's only twenty-one years old; she's a child prodigy. And she's an author of three books already. Shirley was diagnosed with severe juvenile rheumatoid arthritis at only eleven months old. Due to years of hospitalization, she received no schooling until age eleven. Having achieved grade level in all areas after merely 180 days in a special ed class in the elementary school, she was transferred to a regular sixth grade class in middle school. Unfortunately, Shirley lost her eyesight at the age of seventeen. After a successful eye surgery, she hopes to earn science doctorates from Harvard University. Good evening, how are you, Shirley?"

"Hi, Maxine, I'm fine, thank you. How are you?"

"All right. I told you that you have such a little girl voice."

Shirley giggled. "Thank you for having me on the show today."

"Oh, thank you for coming on the show. Your story and your books and your life story in itself is just an inspiration to all people, writers and non-writers."

"Thank you."

"Oh, yes, you've got to tell everyone about—you know, how you keep yourself going and how you write and how you've overcome, you know, how you are able to use a computer. Explain that to me again how you use your computer?"

"Well, I use a software called a screen reader. It reads me what's on the screen and tells me which keys I hit." Shirley was more than grateful to be living in times of technological advances, for JAWS had enabled her to become an author when it would have otherwise been impossible. Because of the severe juvenile rheumatoid arthritis that had made a home in her body since she was eleven months old, she could not use Braille. She had no one to whom she could dictate her writing; her mother's English was not the greatest and she was usually either too tired or too busy. Shirley could record her work using a tape recorder, but it would be hectic, thus taking the fun out of writing. Therefore, without truly enjoying what she did, she would not have decided to become a professional writer. With JAWS, she could write whenever her heart desired as often as she wanted.

Maxine wanted to know how Shirley had become an author, asking her about her first book. Shirley explained that it started with a writing contest sponsored by *Poughkeepsie Journal*, the largest local newspaper in her area. She submitted an expanded version of a story she wrote when she was seventeen for her high school's creative writing class titled *The Magical Gifts*. Afterward, she ended up writing the sequel to the story, for she could not stop thinking about the characters and story line. "By the time I knew it, I wrote eight short stories in the same series," she said. Those stories would become her first book, Daring Quests of Mystics, and she decided to publish it at the same time that her mother suggested that she publish them in one book.

Later into the interview, Maxine said, "Shirley's going to have her mother read from her book, *Dance with Your Heart*. Is your mother available?"

"Oh, yes, she's right here. Her name is Juliet Cheng. And I already have two poems and an excerpt picked out." Shirley handed the receiver over to Juliet, who cleared her voice before speaking.

"Hi, Maxine," came Juliet's almost shy greeting.

"Hi, how are you, Juliet?"

"Good, thank you. How are you?"

"Fine. I just want to commend you on the fight that you had to put up for your daughter for her medical care. So many parents are passive and afraid of what the doctors say...so that was really brave of you...you were like David...going up against the big giant...congratulations."

"Thank you." Juliet had battled two custody cases against doctors in America over treatment disputes for Shirley. She had refused doctors' advice, and they had responded by taking Shirley away in order to force the unwanted and harmful treatments on her.

After Juliet read two poems, one of which was picked out by Maxine, *Oh, God, Give Us Your Light*, Maxine commented that Shirley's writing was so "precocious and so far ahead of her years" and that she had some beautiful poems.

"Yes," said Juliet.

"I really see a lot of talent in your daughter. I know you're very proud of her. She really is a great writer…a lot of lyricism in her words…" She added that Shirley seemed older than her years and that she never allow anything to be an excuse.

"Never," confirmed Juliet. She was not just proud of Shirley—she was proud of herself for being her mother.

After reading another passage from *Dance with Your Heart*, Juliet said, "Maxine, I prepared something beforehand because of my poor English. May I say a few words?"

"Yes, please go ahead."

"Thank you, Maxine, for giving me this opportunity. All of the things I'm about to say have been in my heart left unsaid for many years. First, I'd like to give my daughter Shirley Cheng three thumbs up. Shirley has striven to overcome overwhelming obstacles since her painful diagnosis of severe juvenile rheumatoid arthritis as an infant that left her wheelchair bound, and blindness since the age of seventeen. But she's more so a victim of falsehoods in the American medical system. She received no education until the age of eleven because of years of hospitalization. Having achieved grade level in all areas after 180 days in special education, she was transferred to a regular sixth grade class in middle school. Ever since, she has been a high honor student with straight A's. I think Shirley deserves credits for having survived her various ordeals and that her inexhaustible fortitude, sheer strength, tenacious spirit, and outstanding efforts in her various academic and personal achievements should leave people inspired and touched. But rather, Shirley had been frequently victimized by the American hospital psychologists who had falsely claimed her as being defective, which has had an adverse influence on the course of therapy. After so many years, the evidence is clear enough, more than sufficient, that Shirley is just exactly opposite from the picture those psychologists had painted. Shirley has many outstanding qualities that many would admire. She's one of the most confident, competitive, optimistic, responsible, highly motivated and delightful individuals, with a variety of talents and interests, and has strong character and colorful personality. The happiness she gives is exquisite. Indeed, Shirley is a miracle, a magic gift, a child prodigy, a star with endless shine, and should be known as a role model to the society. Thank you, Maxine."

***

"Are you kidding?" Shirley could not believe that her mother would actually think they could go to New York City. "It will be so hard for us—you know that!"

"Yes, it will be very hard, but it's for your own good. I know it will be very hard, but I can do it," Juliet insisted.

"We'd have to take so much stuff. We'd even have to bring the commode," argued Shirley.

"I'll just pack everything in the van."

"And you'd have to carry me so many times!" Shirley shook her head. The more she thought of it, the more unlikely it seemed possible. She knew the health condition they were both in, especially Juliet. She did want to attend BookExpo America 2005 very much, but she had to be sensible—sensible for her mother's sake. She knew that Juliet often pushed herself to the edge for her. "It starts on June 4—that's when I'll have my period!"

"How about we decide then? If you won't have it then, we'll go, if you do, we'll stay."

"All right," Shirley reluctantly agreed. Her reddie, as she called it, was already too messy to care for at home; she could not imagine having it in the hotel. Plus, she sometimes had bad cramps, followed by nausea if they got severe.

It was only February, so they had plenty of time to prepare for the trip. But first, it was time for her book signing, which was coming up in just a few days. Shirley had been much too impatient for it to arrive. The signing would be held during the Chinese New Year party, which was sponsored by their community's Chinese association, to celebrate the Year of the Rooster at a high school not too far from their home. She had ordered plenty of her books, and Juliet had made a poster with "Book Signing" across the top in large writing. The bright green sign just listed the books' titles, with Chinese translations next to each title. They would have someone stay with them to push Shirley and help them with anything that happened to come up. Shirley's best friend Erin and Erin's boyfriend would attend the event, which would be filled with stage performances and Chinese traditional music. Shirley would have a blast, she was certain.

Indeed, Shirley was having a grand time when the big day knocked on their door. Shirley wore her favorite pink dress and a pretty white crochet top. She sat behind the table on which her books lay. She and the other vendors, who sold canned soda and Chinese munchies, occupied the lobby, where dinner tickets were also sold. She nor Juliet planned to eat anything during the event, which was to end around ten in the evening. They never ate when they attended any event, so this was no different. Shirley was usually too excited to have hunger for food; satisfying her craving for fun and excitement was sufficient to keep her full. In actuality, Shirley was a small eater; she had had a severe lack of appetite ever since she was five months old. Back then, a family member, Agatha, had cared for her for a week. It was not the least bit of care, as Juliet had soon sadly learned. The then-five-month-old Shirley had nearly lost all of her muscle mass when the week of "care" was up, and had seldom hungered for food ever since. Then Juliet found out that Shirley had a serious parasitic infestation, which she had been trying to get rid of to no avail. Only Agatha's neglect could have caused the parasitic infestation, because Juliet had always been overly clean with Shirley, and had sterilized her baby bottles by boiling them in pots daily without failing.

Shirley knew how good it felt to be hungry and to quench the hunger with food she loved, but hunger was seldom a feeling she had the privilege to experience; most days, she mechanically ate in order to survive. She could go for days without food; she simply was sick and tired of eating, and wished that she could live without food. It was not simply a lack of appetite; the trouble went deeper. When she did not want to eat something, or sometimes, even when she did want to eat something, the food would nauseate her; it was a symptom of her parasitic infestation. Her nausea had subsided greatly as she got older; she used to vomit when she was little. Ever since her appetite loss at five months old, Juliet had fed her until around the age of eleven, spending hours on the task daily.

Juliet knew that if she had not, Shirley would have been long gone. However, the constant feeding had badly damaged Juliet's neck permanently.

"I'd like to have your mom's autograph, too," a kindly-looking woman requested. She greatly admired Juliet, who was a role model mother.

Shirley laughed. "Of course!" She passed her pen to Juliet.

"What should I write?" Juliet asked to no one in particular, giggling.

"You can write 'Happy Chinese New Year' in Chinese," Shirley suggested. Juliet did so on the copyright page of the book; Shirley always signed on the dedication page, with a short message specific for a title. She wrote "Never fear of dreaming big..." for *Daring Quests of Mystics*; "Hope builds strong wings..." for her autobiography; and "A dancing heart teaches true" would accompany her autograph for *Dance with Your Heart*.

By the end of the day, Shirley had sold about fifteen copies of her books; she lost count toward the end, for most people bought a copy after the stage performances were over and before heading out of the school building. Shirley quickly estimated how much she had received and was glad to know she had made over one hundred dollars, but after Juliet paid their assistant and his mother, whom he had brought along, ninety dollars, and after paying for their dinner tickets, all of Shirley's profit was given away. Obviously, her book signings would never be profitable, only fun, if they always needed someone to help them. Shirley wondered who would ever help someone without pay, or at least with less pay. Where were all the volunteers who helped in the community? Oh, yes, she was not "the community" but just an individual, so helping her without pay was not as rewarding.

# Chapter 999
# Sweet-Bearing Pain

"Are we there, yet?" Shirley knew she sounded like those kids in the commercials impatient to arrive at their destination, but she did not care. She knew they could have gotten there twenty minutes earlier, but thanks to the infamous city traffic, they were only half way there. She smiled wryly. She was not kidding when she said that the traffic was like a very bad case of pneumonia. How could anyone possibly want to work, let alone live, in this badly congested place? Obviously, millions of people seemed to be immune to this congestion. Sure, there were shops after shops and restaurants after restaurants, but she found no attraction in any place if she could not get to where she wanted to go fast, at least faster than this snail's pace at which they were traveling.

"Weekdays are always like this," sighed Juliet. "It will be better over the weekend. It should be better." Shirley hoped she was right. BookExpo America 2005 was held on Friday June 4 to Sunday June 6, so they would have only one day of bad traffic experience, hopefully. Shirley had decided to attend the event when she was certain that her reddie would not interfere with their trip.

"Gee," said Juliet a moment later. "What now?"

"What's wrong?"

"The road is blocked. I have to turn to the left as

the police have directed." Shirley knew what that meant: if the new route would bring them to the Jacob K. Javits Conventional Center, they would be lucky; if not, then too bad—they would just have to spend who knew how many extra minutes on the road. To their delight, they made it to the center ten minutes later.

"A four-minute drives lasts over thirty minutes! This is ridiculous." But Shirley was glad they were finally there. For probably the fifth time that morning, she mentally checked what she planned to do as Juliet pushed her toward the building. She wanted to sell publishing rights to her three books, and had her media kits ready. She did not bring all forty of them, as that would be too much for them to manage. She was thankful that it was very warm, so she did not need to wear heavy winter attire that would have taken up plenty of space. She also planned to meet Christopher Paolini, the bestselling author of *Eragon* who was about nine months younger than she. She had never read his book, but she had asked her Braille and Talking Book Library to send her the audio tape of his work when they finished recording it.

"We have to get our badges," Shirley reminded her mother. "You have the printouts, right?"

"I know. I'm taking you to get them." She handed Shirley the registration printouts.

Fifteen minutes later, they received their badges and were free to explore the convention center as they pleased, but Shirley knew that they could not go around the place too much, for the floor had carpeting, very heavy carpeting in some areas, and it would be hard for Juliet to push her heavy power wheelchair, especially when Juliet's hands hurt her quite a bit. Juliet had been working hard at home, caring for both their house and Kwi Show, and had abandoned caring for herself. As a result, she had overworked herself to the point that her hands suffered greatly. They had moved together to a new house in 2003, and Juliet had been overworking ever since. Why did Shirley not use a manual wheelchair instead? They had always hung on to their hope of having Shirley see very soon, so she could continue driving her power wheelchair.

They went by booth after booth. Shirley held several media kits in her hands, hoping that some large New York publisher would magically appear in front of her and ask to buy the rights to her books. The wish of every author is recognition for their work, so they could touch one life at a time. Shirley knew the competition was great: there are about 160,000 books published annually in the United States, so it is impossible for everyone to become well known. However, with plenty of passion and faith, not to mention time, effort, work and patience, it would not be impossible to make a difference to the world, one book at a time.

Afternoon quickly arrived, and soon it was time to meet Christopher. He was to sign at the autographing area. Shirley had some pizza before they went to his table to meet him. The line of people waiting to get an autographed copy of his forthcoming release *Eldest* clearly confirmed his fame; the line stretched seemingly endlessly. "It's the longest line in the world," Shirley heard one say.

Shirley was excited about meeting the young author. She gave him her business card when her turn to meet him finally arrived. "I know your dad," she told him.

"Oh, you do?"

"Yes, I wrote to him." She had briefly exchanged messages with him on the forum dedicated to *Eragon*, expressing admiration for Christopher's achievements. "I wrote this book," she said, holding out her 700-page autobiography.

"Wow, that's a thick book!"

"Will you be at the authors luncheon tomorrow?" Shirley wanted to know, hoping that his answer would be yes. She wanted to get a chance to talk with him. It was not every day that she got to meet a famous author, especially one in her age group.

"No, he won't," answered the woman sitting next to him. Shirley guessed that she was his literary agent.

Shirley thanked him for the book before Juliet pushed her away. "I hope you'll enjoy reading my book," he added, not knowing that Shirley was blind.

Mother and daughter then visited the International Rights Center, where book professionals bought and sold foreign to film rights. They asked several people about buying rights, but all of them said that they were selling rights. Shirley had no luck there because the people there had appointments, and she had no literary agent to represent her. Most traditional publishers, especially the larger publishing companies, require that authors have literary agents; they do not accept unsolicited manuscripts. So mother and daughter decided to call it a day and left the center.

One day down, two to go, not that Shirley was counting down the event days as though they were duties they needed to complete, but it was indeed exhausting, especially for Juliet. They would return Saturday at a later time, since Shirley had reserved a luncheon table for both of them and they had no plans prior.

The next morning, Shirley was the first to wake up, not the first time, but heaven knew how many times. She had not slept well. She had developed an ache inside her mouth before arriving in the city, and the pain had rapidly intensified, so it had bothered her throughout the night. In addition, so many shrieking fire trucks had invaded the night that it seemed as though the city was on fire quite a few times. The clanks and clunks of something outside added to the crescendo. Now Shirley understood why they called it the city that never slept. Plus, the rock-hard bed did not help her get her beauty sleep, either. *Forget about sleeping in this city*, she thought.

As she thought of what she would do at the center, Juliet stirred. She was sleeping at Shirley's feet; she had no room to sleep next to Shirley, for Shirley was surrounded with six pillows and six bed sheets, all supporting her bent arms and legs. They had asked for a king-sized bed but were given a double-sized one instead. The plus side to the hard bed was that it did not sag, so every inch of it was "usable," as Juliet had put it.

"You are awake?" Juliet asked quietly when she saw Shirley swinging her legs from side to side. Shirley often swung her legs ever since she could remember; it felt comfortable because her legs could feel restless without doing so.

"Yes."

"Did you sleep well?"

Shirley groaned in answer. "How about you?"

"I slept all right, but I didn't sleep long. I was up for most of the night." Juliet checked her watch and noticed that they would have to work fast to get to the center in time for the authors luncheon. But she had to lie there for just another minute.

"Okay, we'd have to get going," Juliet sighed a minute later. "Are you sure you don't want any breakfast? They're still serving it," she said for what seemed like the third time.

"No, I'll have something to eat at the luncheon."

Juliet tiredly rose from the bed. Her body mechanically moved as her head was still groggy. She got out what they were to wear. She put socks on Shirley and helped her urinate before she sat her up to brush her teeth.

"You should at least drink something," urged Juliet.

"No," came Shirley's answer, the answer Juliet expected but not hoped for. Shirley never drank anything before going out for an event where she would be away from her bedpan for an extended period of time. She would rather be thirsty than have a bladder that was about to burst. "Mom, you should really eat something."

"No," said Juliet. It, too, was the answer Shirley expected yet not hoped for. Juliet had developed an unexplainable torturous medical condition ever since she took one capsule of a weight-loss prescription medication—a drug not prescribed for her but which was cajoled into taking by Agatha, even though Juliet was slim then. She had quite rapidly gained forty pounds afterward, suffering severe water retention. It had been five years already; she had agonizingly spent every minute. If you could not breathe well every single day and night for five years, and if you had to constantly be extra careful of what you ate or drank—any time you did not eat or drink "right" would result in extreme difficulty in breathing (and yet even if something you think is "right" might still result in a bad reaction)—would you not be in agony, too? Sometimes, Juliet could not eat or drink what she wanted, or would eat or drink something she did not want, in order to have the ability to have "okay" breathing. One has to be in her shoes to understand this mysterious condition, a tightness in her diaphragm area, not involving her lungs in any way. Therefore, Juliet did not eat anything this morning.

Juliet handed Shirley the toothbrush she packed with them. If one looked at the stuff they had brought, one would think that they were traveling to China, not just two hours away from home for an event.

Shirley accepted her toothbrush with her left hand, taking it between her thumb and index finger. Her right arm was immobile at a ninety-degree angle — it could neither straighten nor bend — so she had to use her left hand to do anything that required reaching her head, but her left arm was also bent at a ninety-degree angle, even though it could bend further. Her thumb and index finger on her left hand were the only straight fingers she had, so she had to hold everything either between her thumb and her palm or between her thumb and her index finger, which could not bend at all. She always looked as though she was pointing at somewhere mysterious.

Juliet held a cup of water to her lips, and she used it to rinse her mouth. She spit out the dirty water into an empty cup in Juliet's other hand. Shirley always brushed her teeth twice with rinsing in between.

After Shirley finished brushing her teeth, Juliet began dressing her. She was to wear her silky pink dress with laces. Since both of her arms were bent, it was difficult dressing her. Juliet was always extremely careful so as not to hurt her. Usually, her right arm would go in the article of clothing first, or her head would go in followed by her arms, which Shirley could not raise high. With this particular pink dress, her head would go in first. It was a two-piece outfit, so after Shirley got the top on, she lay down on the bed so her mother could slip on the skirt over her pants. Since Shirley was always either sitting or lying down, she had poor circulation and got cold easily. She always wore pants underneath her dresses or skirts, yet she never wore pants alone. People knew she liked to dress "girlie."

Once Juliet was done dressing her, she carried her onto the wheelchair, using much effort because both the pain in her hands and her breathing difficulty greatly made the task much harder; she had quite easily carried Shirley before she had taken that one deadly capsule. Next, Juliet dressed herself.

Shirley pouted, waiting for Juliet to apply some lipstick onto her full cherry-like lips. It was the only makeup she ever wore, and it was only for special occasions. She liked being natural as much as possible. She put on her ring and bracelet, and Juliet put on her clip-on earrings for her. "You look beautiful, as always!" gushed Juliet, giving her a soft pat on the cheek.

Then the pair was all set to go.

Juliet was correct: the traffic was much less dense than the prior day. It took them less than fifteen minutes to arrive at the center. They went straight into the building this time since they already had their badges. "Where's the special hall for the authors luncheon?" Juliet asked a woman, who pointed somewhere up ahead.

To Shirley's dismay, they had missed lunch, not that she was very hungry; she just wanted something to munch on. "You should have eaten something at the hotel," said Juliet. Shirley just shook her head. "Well, let me take some photos for you then." Juliet rose from her seat and snapped a few photos. Then an Asian woman at their table offered to take a photo of them both, and Juliet graciously accepted.

The luncheon event soon ended and everyone filed out. "Let's go to the publishers' booths," suggested Shirley. "I'll see if any of them would like to publish my books." They had brought several copies of Shirley's books and kept them in the battery compartment behind the wheelchair. The heavy batteries were taken out so the wheelchair could be easier to push, yet it was still heavy. Shirley had already given away some of her books to a few publishers that expressed an interest in them. She planned to follow up with them after a month. Following up is a crucial step in the book business, as every professional is already inundated with work, so it is up to each individual author to check in with others.

"No, you should eat something first."

After some consideration, Shirley nodded. She did feel hungry now. "I'll have the same pizza I had yesterday." The ache in her mouth had worsened since morning, so she used only the right side of her mouth to chew. They had some small talk with the woman occupying their table.

"So why are you here?" asked the woman, after explaining her own reason for attending the event.

"Well, I'm an author," supplied Shirley, handing

her a business card.

"Oh?" The woman raised a brow.

"And I'm her mother." Juliet giggled. She was registered for free as Shirley's guest.

"Well, good luck with everything," the woman said to them before she left, and Shirley returned her well wishes.

As planned, the pair visited some booths before leaving the center.

On the last day of BookExpo America 2005, Shirley met more publishers to whom she gave her books. "Wow, this is absolutely amazing!" exclaimed a gentleman at a large publishing house, looking over her books. "We only publish little kids books, but I'll certainly tell others about you. Do you have some cards I can give others?"

"Thank you!" Shirley handed him a small pile of her business cards and a few media kits. She kept talking to a minimum, for the ache in her mouth had grown into a full-blown throbbing pain. She could barely open her mouth, and talking had been very difficult. She had also skipped breakfast and did not plan to eat anything for the day; it was much too painful to even swallow her saliva.

The man laughed. "I see you have everything prepared."

Later on, Shirley met a woman at the Random House booth. "You are blind?" Astonishment peppered her question. "If you didn't tell me, I would not have known!"

"I try my best," explained Shirley, referring to eye contact.

The woman, as with other publishers, told her that she would need a literary agent to represent her, and said that the gentleman standing beside her happened to be an agent. Therefore, Shirley handed the man a copy of each of her books.

With nothing else to do after visiting all the publishers, Juliet and Shirley ended their adventures at their first BookExpo America attendance. "I'm driving you home today," said Juliet. She could clearly tell that Shirley was not well, being that she had not slept much at the hotel, with all the noise outside and the hard bed; and that she had barely eaten anything, and was suffering from severe constipation and allergies. Shirley only nodded. Even though she could hardly keep her eyes open, she wanted to get back home as soon as possible. Spending another sleepless night would only make her worse. Once home, she would drink some prune juice; she felt terribly bloated. The milk of magnesium, which she had taken daily during their hotel stay, did not ease her constipation but only made her more uncomfortable. Good thing she did not have reddie; that would surely be the cherry on top of an undesirable ice-cream sundae.

Yet they had made it, and that was all that mattered.

# *Are You Unstoppable?*
## How You Can Effectively Conquer Negativity in Five Simple Ways

What does it take for a child to laugh through tears of unimaginable physical pain? How could a student master grade level in all areas after merely 180 days of education in their lifetime? And how could a blind individual write and calculate long chemistry equations without the aid of Braille, write and publish several books, and design their own Web site?

It only takes a positive attitude for a child in pain to laugh. It is possible for a student to devour knowledge with the desire to be their best. And it is from the passion for life where the perseverance comes for a blind person to achieve what seems to be impossible to accomplish without eyesight.

How would I know? I know because I was that child laughing; I was that student hungering for knowledge; and I was that blind author writing and publishing three books by her twenty-first birthday.

After coming out as a winner, I have acquired the secrets to moving forward despite seemingly insurmountable challenges. I have achieved my gold medals, and now, I am ready to hold your hand to guide you down your rugged journey, gently showing you how to choose which roads to travel, so that you, too, can go for your own gold medals in life.

Life is full of obstacles and challenges; you would be fooling yourself to think otherwise. Before we run into any obstacle, we first need to prepare ourselves for negative or challenging situations. We need a cushion on which we can fall back when we run into life's hardships. Think about the acrobats performing in circuses: While they dazzle their audience with their skill and agility, nets below are ready to catch them if they ever fall. This is the kind of protection we need in life, so we will not become badly bruised once we crash down. This protection in life should be gratitude. Appreciation is the essential net to cushion us from ordeals, from everyday obstacles to life's traumas.

Start everything with appreciation. Before you do anything new, say anything new, go anywhere new, meet anyone new, first appreciate your current state in every aspect. This acts like a cushion in the event that your actions return you to your original state. Therefore, if you are thankful for now, when you return to now, you will be thankful that you have not lost anything and will be extra grateful for everything you do gain. So it is vital to appreciate your situation at every stage of your life.

When you run into an obstacle, take the following steps to overcome it.

- **Calm down so you can focus on what you want to achieve.** Your problem requires more attention than your emotions, so give it the spotlight it deserves by putting your emotions aside. What can you do to deal with your situation? Focus your energy on how to improve your situation, not on how you are reacting to it. What might be the best actions to take in order to overcome your obstacle? What positive outcome do you want? You must think outside your fear or negative emotions, so the first step to take is to calm down and put your feelings aside.

Emotions are powerful stuff, and if you do not use them correctly, they will turn your hill into a mountain. Many times, your feelings amplify your situation, making your problems seem too large to handle. Negative emotions, such as worry, doubt, and fear, can put your values, beliefs, and desires in the background, and will glue you to one spot, making you unable to think rationally. Fear, for example, holds you back, prevents you from examining your problem, stops your thoughts and actions, and brings only unbalanced emotions and spirit. If you remove fear from your spirit, you will be able to examine your problem as is, and then you can identify the area that is giving you difficulty.

For example, imagine that a close friend has passed away. You are feeling as though your world is falling apart. You cannot eat; you cannot sleep. All you can do is engulf yourself in your sorrow. You feel as though you cannot live without your friend. Now put your emotions aside for a moment, and examine the facts of your situation:

a) Yes, your friend has passed away, but everyone must meet this end sooner or later. It is reality.

b) You *are* able to live without your friend; of course, you will miss him or her immensely. Think about the time before you and your friend first met. You lived then without this friend, did you not? So it is not impossible to live without him or her now.

c) Life moves on; it is best to move on with it. Your friend would want you to move forward. Appreciate the time you and this friend were together; cherish the happy memories you built together.

Please note that I said that if you use emotions

incorrectly, they will give you trouble. It then follows, of course, that if you use your emotions correctly, they will help you. Let me give you a personal example. My mother Juliet Cheng lost custody of me twice in the United States after refusing unwanted and harmful treatments. She had to battle two horrifying custody cases against doctors in order to protect my life. Fortunately, she won both cases, so I did not receive the treatments that would have sent me to my grave. She was able to win because she used her emotions correctly. Instead of going insane with fright and worry, letting her emotions control her mind and actions, she converted any negative feelings—anger and fright—into positive emotions and energy: determination and willpower. She was definitely in control.

Here is another personal example:

When I lost my eyesight at the age of seventeen, I first focused on making the most of my situation and moving forward. I did not let negative emotions control me. I knew that it was not the end of my life, and that being miserable would not help me in any way. In fact, it would only make my situation worse. Imagine that you are marooned on a deserted island. Would you simply stand there, stomp your feet, pull your hair, and cry "Oh, poor, poor me!"? Would you not instead calm down to think? I also knew that losing my eyesight could be a lot worse than simply that. With this thought, I was actually able to appreciate my situation. I simply did my best with what I had. So I became an author of three books at age twenty, and now at age twenty-four, I am an award-winning author and motivational speaker, with more than seven published books, to touch others with humor, hope, and healing. I may not be able to paint or draw now, but I am still able to love the life I live.

- **Fight negativity with negativity.** Your situation could be a lot worse. Imagine something a lot worse than what you are going through now, and compare these situations—with which situation would you rather be dealing? Instead of losing a friend, you could have lost your entire family. Instead of breaking an arm, you could have broken a leg. Instead of losing your wallet, you could have lost your home to the subprime mortgage crisis that is shaking our economy.
- **Fight negativity with positivity.** Think about something that you are grateful for, that makes you happy, that you love, and then replace your negative thought with the positive one.

Whenever I run into a stressful situation, I think about my Heavenly Father and my beloved earthly mother, and I become so grateful and happy to have them that I no longer find my situation stressful; I am able to tolerate and endure the negativity so much better.

- **Keep these points in mind as you face your obstacle:**

a) There is always someone out there who is in a much worse situation than you, so be thankful for your own situation, for what you have and the people who are around you. While you may be frustrated paying your bills, there are many who are homeless and who would be more than glad to own the keys to your house. While you are complaining about having a bad hair day, at least one person on Earth is losing all of his or her hair while receiving chemotherapy for the cancer that has spread.

b) You are not enduring adversity alone.

Millions and millions of people are suffering this very minute, from the starving in Africa and the homeless on the streets to the abused behind closed doors. And there may be people going through the same difficulty you are experiencing now.

c) Everything passes, and so will your current negative situation. When you are angry or upset, keep in mind that it will pass, so why waste your energy on something that will be gone tomorrow? It is true that a negative event, or any kind of event for that matter, can affect your entire life, but you cannot control life when it shouts "Surprise!" in an unpleasant way. You simply have to prepare for any challenges and make the most of what you have. For instance, the tuberculin skin test I received when I was eleven months old caused the severe juvenile rheumatoid arthritis that will remain with me for the rest of my life. I know that life moves on no matter what happens to me, so it is wise to move along with it and make the best of what I have. Would sulking and worrying about my life do me any good or turn my situation around?

- **Have faith.** Lastly, the most important shield you need to have deep in your heart to fight negativity is faith. The most vital kind of faith is unwavering faith in Jehovah God. Do you think that my mother won her custody cases just by using positive emotions? That was not all—she had a faith in God so strong that no one and nothing could take it from her. And it is faith in God that has allowed me to move forward, one sure step at a time, as I know He is there guiding me, supporting me, and loving me. Keep your faith in God strong and steady, and your steps will be strong and steady in turn.

As you can see, you *can* be in control of what

happens to you after negativity suddenly says "Boo!" in your face. You do not need to be the victim of your troubles. Let your troubles be victims of your faith and positivity. If you do not let problems stop you, they cannot and will not stop you. Only you have the power to stop yourself. It is completely up to you — would you want to be stopped or unstoppable? I made my decision a long time ago. How would you like to join me?

# Chapter IV
# Be the Star You Are!

"It must have been my wisdom tooth," speculated Shirley a week later. She had fasted for fifty-two hours after returning home. The pain was now manageable, and the swelling was almost gone. "I'm lucky; it could have given a lot more trouble than just pain." She had read some horror stories about wisdom teeth, and had not looked forward to getting them. Although no tooth came out, she could not think of anything else that could have caused the excruciating pain. She did not remember biting on the inside of her cheek by accident or hurting her teeth or gum in any way. Not all wisdom teeth come out, so perhaps it was the same case with her.

Enough about wisdom teeth; she had a much more exciting subject to take up her concentration: a radio interview on *Starstyle – Be the Star You Are!* with host Cynthia Brian, radio/television personality and New York Times bestselling author. She was to appear on her show for one twenty-minute segment on Wednesday, August 3. She had had a wonderful experience with her first radio interview, and she was excited about her second. She thought it was about time to have another interview.

***

"She's blind and physically disabled, yet she has authored three books by the age of twenty-one. And she has her eyes set on graduating from Harvard. Meet this role model for today's youth—coming right up on *Starstyle – Be the Star You Are!* She's an inspiration."

Shirley's heart pounded loudly, nearly drowning out Cynthia Brian's melodic voice in the telephone. August 3 had swiftly arrived, and even though she had barely slept the previous night, along with many nights prior, her excitement fueled her with energy. Her segment would start in about a minute after a couple of commercials.

When Cynthia came back on air, Shirley grew more excited, if that was even possible.

"Well, you're listening to *Starstyle – Be the Star You Are!* with me, your personal growth expert, Cynthia Brian. Our next guest is the most perseverant person I have ever met. And she is an excellent promoter and marketeer all the time being very polite yet extremely persistent. What amazed me about this author is that she's just in her early twenties. She's disabled and she's blind, yet she's so optimistic and positive, and accomplished more than most people thrice her age.

This remarkable young woman's books include..."

Shirley listened as the host introduced her. She felt so welcomed and honored to be on her show and to receive such a warm welcome. "Hi, Cynthia, thank you very much for having me on your show!"

"I am so delighted to finally meet you over the airwaves. You are one incredible young lady."

"Thank you." Shirley expressed her delight in finally talking with her. Cynthia asked Shirley to give a bit of her background to the listener and added, "We can learn a lot from you."

After Shirley shared with the audience parts of her life story and they had briefly discussed them, Cynthia said, "You are very dedicated to your mom," and that it was so unusual nowadays to have parents and their children be so close as Shirley and her mother were. "She's the kind of mom I just adore."

Later into the interview, Cynthia read one of Shirley's poems in *Dance with Your Heart* bearing the same title as the book. "I can just see you flying away!"

"What blows me away...you want to go to Harvard, but you don't want just one major—you want several majors!"

"I love life..." Shirley wanted to learn everything about life as much as she could.

"You just love living...you celebrate everything...God's creations."

"Yes."

"We never hear you complain!"

"I never complain."

"You're just glad to be alive!"

"I smile all the time."

Cynthia then asked her what was the next mountain she wanted to climb.

"The eye surgery." Shirley explained that she still had not have any surgery scheduled yet because, "I still haven't found Dr. Right yet." She wanted a doctor who not only was skillful but also kind and compassionate. She needed someone who could listen to her concerns and answer her questions. She did not want a five-minute appointment followed by the surgery on the next visit. Then Dr. Johnson popped into her head. The rheumatologist who helped Juliet win the 1990 case recently recommended the eye doctor in the New York Eye and Ear Infirmary, and an appointment had been scheduled with him for the following month. Shirley fervently hoped that her search for Dr. Right would end with him.

Cynthia said that she hoped that some incredible eye surgeon would contact Shirley after listening to the show. "You deserve to see again."

In no time, the segment ended. "You have been a fabulous guest. Give a huge, huge hug and bravo to your mom! May we all learn from you."

# Chapter V
# Hunting for Dr. Right

At 9:45 on the morning of September 8, Juliet and Shirley set off to New York City. Shirley's appointment was scheduled for 1:45 that afternoon, but they wanted to give themselves ample time to get to the city and arrive at the doctor's office; it was better to be early rather than late or just on time, so they would not have to rush. The infirmary did not have a parking lot, so they would have to park the van somewhere else, then Juliet would have to push Shirley a few blocks to get to the infirmary; that alone would cost them about half an hour.

On the road, many questions hammered in Shirley's head, as with all her other appointments when visiting new doctors. *Would this doctor be skillful? Would he patiently listen to what I need to say, and would he explain everything to me fully? What kind of person and doctor would he be? Would he be the one who restores my vision?*

They arrived at the parking lot around 11:30. After Juliet pushed Shirley off the van, she pushed her toward the infirmary. She kept on the curbs and told Shirley every time when there was a dent along the way or if she would need to lift her feet a bit to prevent her feet from bumping to any raised area. "Good thing that there are always people walking on the streets in the city," said Shirley, as Juliet asked a gentleman to lift the front of her wheelchair a bit so she could push Shirley onto a higher curb.

When they finally settled down at Dr. Johnson's office, it was noontime. His office was on the third floor, but that day, he was seeing his patients on the fourth floor, so they had to use the elevator again when they did not find him in his usual office.

At precisely 1:45, Shirley's name was called. "That's very punctual," she commented to her mother, who followed a doctor into an examining room. "Is he Dr. Johnson?"

"I don't know," said Juliet.

After situating inside, the doctor turned to them and introduced, "Hi, I'm Dr. Patterson." He was Dr. Johnson's partner, and he would question Shirley and examine her eyes first before her doctor came. "Hmm, this cannot be lowered enough," he said, trying to get the slit lamp down to Shirley's height.

"Yes, we usually run into this problem," said Shirley. "It usually cannot be lowered enough to reach me." Every eye doctor's office, she thought, should have equipment that could be lowered enough to examine wheelchair-bound people. Not every disabled person could be carried. How could the disabled get their eyes examined properly? Last year when she saw a different specialist, she had had to be lifted from her wheelchair a few seconds so they could put thick telephone-like books on her seat on which to sit. It was the least comfortable way to have an examination.

"Let's see if we can have people carry you onto the chair."

"Is there any room that has one that can be lowered?" asked Juliet. A local eye doctor Shirley saw back in May had had only one that could be lowered enough.

"Unfortunately, we don't," replied Dr. Patterson.

That was when Dr. Johnson walked in and promptly introduced himself, shaking both Juliet's and Shirley's hands.

"You are Dr. Johnson?" Surprise tinted Juliet's question.

"I am older than I look." He smiled.

From his voice, Shirley instantly relaxed several notches. He sounded very kind. Yes, she depended on voices a lot to determine people's nature and disposition. Voices can tell a lot about people.

"So what is your reason for coming?" Dr. Johnson asked Shirley when he seated himself in front of her.

"I would like to get different opinions," answered Shirley. She wanted to gather enough information from eye doctors and get her questions answered to make her final decision.

He managed to examine her eyes as she remained in her wheelchair craning her neck and lifting her behind. He used low light after she told him she was very photophobic. "You know all the terms." He laughed. After a brief examination, he turned away the equipment.

"First of all, the cataract surgery itself is trivial; any decent eye doctor can perform it. What is the most important thing is to get any inflammation under control. Because of the nature of the autoimmune disease, JRA, and also uveitis, you could develop inflammation from the surgery," he explained. He suggested that Shirley be on a medicine that could prevent that from happening. If Shirley got an inflammation after a successful surgery, she could lose her eyesight again, and this time, it would be serious. "You should take the medicine for three months prior to the surgery and stay on it a few months afterward." He prescribed CellCept. Both Juliet and Shirley had just previously told Dr. Patterson about Shirley having severe reactions as a result of taking methotrexate and even aspirin. Shirley was concerned about CellCept, and made a mental note to read about it on the Internet when she returned home. He further told her that if she did not follow his advice to take any medicine, he would not operate on her. "You could also just see me to control the inflammation if not for the surgery itself. But I advise you to find a local eye doctor because if something comes up after the surgery and you would need to see the doctor right away, you would not be able to make it all the way to the city to see me."

"We will stay in a hotel if Shirley has the surgery here," supplied Juliet.

"Okay, but she would need regular check ups after the surgery."

Shirley felt quite good about what she heard from him. "You've been the only one so far—out of all the eye doctors I have seen—to tell me all this." She felt what he said made a lot of sense and fully agreed with his concerns. "What do you think of lens implantation for me?"

"Implanting a lens in your eye could cause an inflammation. So if you don't mind, I suggest glasses or contact lenses."

"Contact lenses would be too difficult for me to put on," said Shirley. They could hurt her sensitive eye—her right eye, since it was the eye she wanted to get operated on, and Dr. Johnson agreed, for it was the eye that could potentially see after cataract extraction; vision loss on her left eye was caused by band keratopathy. He was also the only eye doctor who said she should not have the lens implanted in her eye.

"Give the matter some thought. Do not make any decision right away," said Dr. Johnson. "You can call me or Dr. Patterson if you have any questions." No one had ever offered that before!

After he left the room, Dr. Patterson examined Shirley's eyes, shining bright light. He put numbing eyedrops in her eyes in order to perform the pressure test.

"I get hurt after doctors do the pressure," said Shirley, hoping that he would not perform it. "My eyes are very sensitive. I often got hurt for days afterward." She then handed him her business card.

"Are you a philosopher? I would like to talk to you sometimes on the phone and you can teach me some philosophy." he said. " I can see that you're very smart—you look smart."

"You can tell?" questioned Juliet, giggling. How many times had she heard that from Asians?

Shirley laughed. "Sure…thank you."

The doctor turned to Juliet. "You're a great mother. Shirley has been cared for very well."

They ended Shirley's appointment at 3:15, and Dr. Patterson had either forgotten or decided not to perform the pressure test on her, and that greatly relieved her. For the very first time after a doctor's appointment, both Juliet and Shirley felt happy. Shirley did not leave disappointed, unhappy, or ticked off, unlike previous visits to eye doctors. Most doctors did not say anything to Shirley, whereas some others treated her with a poor attitude.

Shortly after returning home at 6:30 that evening, Shirley signed on to the Internet to research CellCept. Shirley was immensely disappointed when she finished the search. "The medicine is used for patients who will receive transplants to prevent their bodies from rejecting the foreign body. It causes infections because it suppresses the immunity, and it can even cause tumor growth," she told her findings to Juliet. Shirley was positive that she could not take it. An otherwise healthy person with a nutritional and balanced diet would be able to take the medicine. Since Shirley had a very poor appetite and was, in turn, anemic, she would not be able to withstand it.

"I told you so," Juliet said. How right she was.

So now, Shirley was going to continue seeing doctors locally. It was not wise to make far travels to the city when anything came up after the surgery. And they decided to forget about CellCept for now, until she was strong enough to take it.

# Chapter VI
# The Tough Getting Tougher

The autumn days grew cooler when November approached. Shirley had been spending her days thinking of ways to tie her books in with news headlines. "The media is not interested that you have a book; they want to know if you can offer a good segment that will give them a high rating," was what she often heard. She knew she had many good angles, but tying them in with national news could be tricky. Then she thought of parental rights in children's medical care, a serious issue in which both Juliet and she had been directly affected. Why not make the society, specifically the parents, aware of this matter? Not only would advocating this help her tie her autobiography (which covers and reveals many important issues concerning their society) in with the news—there happened to be a custody case currently in the headlines—it would most importantly be a great cause about which she felt strongly. She had not only the desire, but also the responsibility, to help others in the society. She could not let the problems her mother and she had been forced to withstand happen to other people in the future. Being disabled was already hard enough without having to endure all the unnecessary manmade hardships. She strongly believed that by uniting their power, they could move mountains, and turn their country into a true nation run by the people for the people.

Thus, she devoted part of her time writing her arguments, show ideas, and pitches, and delivering them to appropriate media. One of these days, she would have enough material to write a book dedicated to protecting parental rights and helping parents and children be heard.

Besides focusing on the parental rights issue, she also directed inspirational story ideas to the media, including much faith and passion in her pitches. Her pitch had even made one major magazine editor cry. A television producer told her that she had a perfect pitch. What more could they ask from her? If they wanted inspirational stories, she was the ideal person to be interviewed. What kind of empowering stories did they want? When would they get tired of celebrity stories? It seemed as though one either had to be a celebrity or a criminal in order to catch the U.S. media's attention.

Shirley had not had much luck getting the media's attention in the United States. Even getting a mention in her local newspapers was hard enough. But she was immediately featured in *World Journal*, the largest Chinese daily newspaper in North America, after Shirley E-mailed them; she did not even have to write a hook or a pitch; they were simply interested in her story as an extraordinary human being. The journalist called Shirley on the same day after receiving her E-mail, and Shirley was interviewed on the spot. The long article, with her prom photograph, came out that Sunday in July 2004. If the American media showed a fraction of interest in people like her, rather than devoting themselves to money and fame like royal puppies, she would not have had to go through all this trouble to pitch them, without getting much result in return.

If the big media folks did not want her now—it was their loss—then too bad. She could always start small and slowly climb upward. At least, the other media, specifically radio shows, were interested in what she had to share. Therefore, on November 2, Shirley had another interview on *Be the Star You Are!* with Cynthia Brian to give more words of inspiration to the audience. Then on the seventh, Stu Taylor invited Shirley to be on his radio show, *Stu Taylor on Business*, on the morning of Thanksgiving Day, for he thought it was the perfect day to have Shirley on as a symbol of true thanksgiving.

That same day in the afternoon, while Shirley was surfing the Internet, her Internet answering machine rang. Her attention was immediately yanked from her when her mother's distraught voice came on the speakers.

"Pearl, I just got into a car accident and—"

Shirley did not wait to hear anything else as she accepted the call, ending her Internet connection. She picked up the telephone when it rang. "Mom, what happened? Are you okay?"

"I'm okay, but the car is not." Juliet went on to explain that the driver behind her smashed into her trunk. "She wasn't paying attention to where she was going, so she smashed right into me. The entire trunk is gone...glass is everywhere..." Juliet then said that she would be speaking to the police, and would get home as soon as she could. She was just a few minutes away from home when the accident occurred. Fortunately, she had been driving slowly, because the car in front of her was about to make a turn, but the woman behind her kept driving, for she was looking somewhere else.

Shirley detected Juliet's breathlessness. Was she really okay? "Mom, are you sure you're okay? You should get checked up."

"No, no, I'm fine. I have to hang up now. I'll be home soon."

"Okay, be careful. I love you."

"I love you, too."

Shirley fervently hoped that her mother was truly as fine as she had insisted. She knew that Juliet never liked seeing doctors, especially having emergency visits when she would have to wait for hours. Once, she had gone to the emergency room, but had left after hours of waiting without seeing any doctor. She was, of course, promptly charged for the visit. Shirley did not have to wonder how Juliet was for long, as Juliet returned home in less than thirty minutes.

"Mom, are you in any pain? Did you break anything?"

"I'm just shaken up, that's all."

Shirley felt uneasy. What if Juliet fell ill later on? Not all symptoms would come out right away. As she had dreaded, Juliet became more than a little uncomfortable that evening: she could not open her jaw when she yawned; her neck and throat felt tight. Shirley urged her to go to the emergency room, but she still refused.

As days passed, Juliet felt a different kind of numbing sensation in her hands, adding to her own numbness and pain. Juliet finally agreed to see a doctor when her no-fault insurance told her that they would pay her medical bills up to fifty thousand dollars. A neurologist performed an EEG and EMG on her. The test results showed that she had nerve damage, including carpal tunnel syndrome, which was caused by her overwork around the house. Much to her annoyance and frustration, her no-fault insurance turned around and refused to pay for her EEG and EMG medical bills, saying that they were medically unnecessary. They also refused to pay for physical therapy. With no choice, Juliet had to stop physical therapy after one homecare visit. She was unable to receive any kind of treatment; her only remedy was hope.

Juliet continued her work as usual, gritting her teeth against the pain and numbness. She did not fail as a good daughter nor as a good mother. She did what she was supposed to do, just as before. In February, she would take Shirley for another book signing at the Chinese New Year party in a different high school, which was much closer to home than the one before. She would have the same man go with them to help her. She needed his help more than ever now.

# Chapter VII
# Good Luck Year of the Dog

Juliet was performing chores one January day when she heard a long squeal. *Pearl must have good news!* she thought. Just as she was about to ask her daughter, an "I won!" invaded the atmosphere. *She won?* "What is it, Pearl?"

"I'm tied for first place in the Be the Star You Are! essay contest!" She had submitted her essay titled *The Jewel from Heavenly Father*, a tribute to her mother.

"I am so thrilled for you!"

"And I get to appear on Cynthia's show on the eleventh. I also will receive fifty dollars." She would have been entitled to receive one hundred dollars if she was the only winner. "The year is starting out really well." Year of the Dog would start on January 23, and since she was a Dog, the year might prove to be lucky to her. This year, she wanted to primarily focus on scheduling book signings at her local bookstores and getting bookstores in other states to stock her books. She would first search for telephone numbers and begin her work from there. The year was also starting out as a busy one; she had four radio interviews scheduled in January, and she had a feeling that many more would follow.

\*\*\*

Dressed in a red blouse and a fuchsia velvety full skirt, Shirley greeted folks at her table during her book signing at the Chinese New Year party. "Happy New Year!" She smiled at a woman who just went over to her table.

"Shirley, I read about you in the *Poughkeepsie Journal*. You are such an inspirational person! I wanted to come to your signing and buy your autobiography." The woman bought two copies, one for herself and one to share with her friends. "You have achieved so much; it's amazing!"

"Thank you! I'm honored that you've come to my signing. I hope you'll enjoy reading my book." Shirley gave the woman another smile before she left. Shirley wondered how many people had read the article in the newspaper. She had sent *Poughkeepsie Journal* a press release of her engagement, and to her delight, they posted an article about her event in the Life section.

Another woman came up to Shirley's table and introduced herself as Margaret, one of her customers from last year who had purchased her autobiography. "I loved your book; it's so beautiful! I couldn't put it down."

"I'm so glad you enjoyed reading it."

"I'd like to buy another one of your books." She ended up purchasing *Daring Quests of Mystics*, while a friend she brought along bought *Dance with Your Heart*.

"You'll really like this book," Juliet told Margaret's friend. "The poems are very good."

"Good, I need some inspirational and relaxing reading!" The woman laughed.

"Next year, you may have new books," said Margaret.

"I may." Shirley was not working on any new book projects of her own; she had been contributing to other people's book projects. Little did she know that in two years, she would be the author of seven books, one of which a multi-award winner, and a contributing author of eleven books, two of which she would co-author with highly acclaimed experts and authors in the self-improvement field.

"You never know!" Margaret then bid her and Juliet a goodbye before leaving. Dinner was about to start. As usual, Juliet and Shirley did not plan to eat anything.

Shirley glowed with happiness all over. Her happiness was for the year that was starting out so well; for being alive to experience the happiness; and for having the privilege and ability to touch others through her books.

A month following her book signing, Shirley received an E-mail from Donald Mitchell, a top ten Amazon.com reviewer, inviting her to contribute to *101 Great Ways to Improve Your Life, Volume 2*, a book that would be compiled by the founder of SelfGrowth.com. A handful of the world's leading experts, such as Jack Canfield, Dr. John Gray, Dr. Richard Carlson, Alan Cohen, and Bob Proctor, were to be among the 101 contributors of the 101 articles, and Shirley could be one of them. *I would be quite honored to be a part of the book project*, thought Shirley, who thoroughly enjoyed contributing to such projects. She immediately contacted SelfGrowth.com to tell them that she would like to submit an article for the book. She so happened to have recently begun a self-empowerment article titled *Dance with Your Heart: How to Befriend Your Heart and the World Around You*, and thought it would be perfect for their project.

Stacy from SelfGrowth.com promptly E-mailed Shirley back with all the necessary information and a contract, which Shirley needed to sign. By the end of the month, Shirley had E-mailed them her article and faxed in the contract. Now all that was left to do was to wait for acceptance. She had never imagined that waiting for approval would be so spine tingling and stomach fluttering. For days, she waited anxiously by her computer for the acceptance E-mail.

She was checking her E-mail on April 11 when her Internet answering machine rang. A few seconds later, Stacy's chippy voice came on and froze Shirley in place. She dared not even breathe.

A loud, long squeal did not fail to escape from the smiling Shirley as soon as Stacy hung up. If she could walk, she would have gotten up and danced there and then. She would have boogie woogied around the entire house and onto the yard. Instead, her heart waltzed to the music of her soul.

Juliet laughed. "I told you that you'd be accepted! Your article is just excellent. I'd be shocked if they didn't want it."

Shirley's glee lasted for days; the days easily turned into weeks. She was still smiling in her soul on May 3, when she received an E-mail from a woman named Janice that bore the subject: John T. Mather Hospital.

> Shirley:
> I am a director, and benefactor of a Breast Center, for John T. Mather Hospital in Port Jefferson, New York (further out on the Island)
> Each year we have a Victory Day Celebration of Breast Cancer Survivors. I try to give inspirational

talks, along with other sponsors of this even. It is NOT a fund raiser but a celebration of the Survivors that starts, via the train - free of charge, at Penn Station and arrives in Port Jefferson at our hospital. The Hospital provides lunch, beverages and generally celebrates all these woman in our area that have breast cancer and are survivors.
I'm asking whether you would be interested in speaking about something inspirational at this event in 2007. Please contact me.
I am obligated to tell you that there would be no compensation for this. It is all voluntary.
Thank you.

This E-mail completely washed away the book project from Shirley's mind. She solely concentrated on the news. She would absolutely love to speak at the event, but how were they able to take the train? Who would carry her on and off the train and taxis? It would be too much for Juliet to handle alone. She could still clearly see in her mind's eye the train trips they had taken in China. They were nightmarish. She vividly recalled one particular incident when Juliet could not get onto the train because the steps were insanely high, and all the passengers were pushing and shoving against her; one even kicked the stroller she held from her hands down to the tracks several feet away from her. The train was just about to leave without her when she pleaded for a fellow passenger to give her a good push. She got on at the last minute, reuniting with the frightened Shirley, who thought that Juliet could never get up and onto the train. Shirley did not know what the situation was like in America, whether trains were high, so she would need to do some research.

Later that day, Shirley wrote Janice back,

expressing her gratitude for the gracious invitation and her interest in attending the event as a guest speaker, but without giving her a definite answer, telling her that she would have to do some research first.

Next, Shirley contacted the train station to find out their accessibility. Within a couple of days, they returned her E-mail with the answers she fervently hoped for—the trains had no steps, and she could be wheeled in directly from the raised platform. They had elevators and people to assist her. Janice also E-mailed her to tell her that they had wheelchair-accessible buses. It did seem that everything would be fine, which meant Shirley would be able to go.

For days, Shirley and Juliet talked about the event to no end. Shirley had even thought of what she was to say in her speech. How thrilled she was! She wished that it were on the following day, not over a year later in September 2007. It was much too long for an excited girl to wait! Too bad they had already chosen the speakers for this year; one speaker would be Senator Hillary Clinton, whom Shirley hoped would be one of the speakers for next year as well.

"Guess what the title of my article is!" Shirley challenged Juliet. They often played guessing games, or rather, Shirley would often torture Juliet in the process of making her guess what she wrote, this time, the title of the article which was her speech for Victory Day; last time, it had been the *Dance with Your Heart* article.

After several guesses, Juliet ventured, "Does it have 'Celebrate' in it?"

"Yes! That's the first word. What are the next seven?" Shirley giggled, joined in by Juliet. After a while, Juliet got the first three words: Celebrate Your

Existence.
>"Okay, you'd have to tell me. I give up."
>"*Celebrate Your Existence, for It Is Your Privilege!*"
>"How nice!"
>"Yes, it is our privilege to live."
>"Indeed."

# Dance with Your Heart

## How to Befriend Your Heart and the World around You

What do you see when people dance? Is it how their hands and feet move so gracefully in such unison with one another, yet each of them sparkles with individuality? Are the dancers smiling? What does that mean? They may be joyous when they move their bodies to the rhythms of the music, but that is not all. They smile because they are dancing with their hearts.

What do I mean when I say they dance with their hearts? When you are dancing with your heart, you are dancing together with your heart and dancing using your heart, and as a result, you are becoming a dancing heart.

What do you feel when you see them dance? Do you feel like dancing as well? When you dance, you will project how you feel and what you feel onto any onlookers, causing them to have a desire, a need, to mirror your feelings, then finally your actions. You set good examples of life when you dance; you are teaching true things of life, so you must lead others by dancing yourself.

To dance with your heart, you must be pure. Release all the negative feelings hammering inside you and block out the ugly voices the outside world whispers stealthily in your ears. Become friends with yourself. What qualities do you look for in a friend?

Are you ready to become your own friend and

dance with your heart? Take the following dance steps on your own before you can hold hands with your heart.

- Acceptance. Accept who you are as a whole. Accept how you feel. Accept how you think. Accept how you look from your head to your toes. You may not like to accept yourself as you are now because you feel you are not perfect. But what is perfection anyway? Is nature perfect? If so, then you must be perfect, too. Take a look—I bet that tall tree in your backyard has at least one torn branch, but is it still majestic? Does it still deserve to be called beautiful? Perfect?
- Openness. Be open, truthful, and honest with yourself. Do not lie to yourself. Do not live with pretense. When something is making you unhappy, face it, do not run away from it. Change the situation with a clear and honest look. By closely examining the situation you are in, you will be able to find the root of the problem and plug it out. By remaining in the dark, you will never find that root, so turn on the lights!
- Understanding. Understand your feelings, thoughts, and why you behave the way you do. Find the purpose to your actions. Learn from your past and those situations that did not go as smoothly as hoped, and utilize what you learn to make your future bright.
- Love and appreciation. Love yourself.

Honestly tell yourself, "I know I am not a bad person. I know I do my best in everything I do, and I know I am being my best, so I love myself because I am a good person with good intentions." Appreciate what you have and whom you have. Appreciate what you are able to do.

- Positivity. Count your blessings. Focus on the good things you do have at the present and the positive side of things. Do not dwell on bad situations, but instead, move forward and have a bright attitude and outlook for the future. You have the ability to make a positive difference to your future just by being positive. Choosing the road to positivity and happiness will give you the strength, the desire, and the motivation to take giant steps forward. Don't pick the road to misery — it will just glue you to one spot, and you wouldn't want to get the glue onto others, now would you?
- Passion. Be passionate about who you are and what you do. Value life; cherish every minute that is given to you. Hold on tightly to the happy moments and their memories because when they're gone, they're gone forever. Live with conviction; live with vitality.
- Happiness. Smile often. Smile to yourself, even if there's no good reason. Smiling will warm you up, even when the days seem dreary. Frequently treat yourself to

a big smile while working or frolicking; it is the sweetest treat you can give yourself, and the best part is that there are no calories!

Once you achieve calm in your soul, you will be able to spiritually connect with your own self from deep within you, and that is where your heart lies.

What is your heart? No, it is not the muscular organ that pumps blood through your body; it is your essence, your higher self or energy. No one has the power to harm your heart, especially if you don't allow outside negativity to pollute your spirit like a thick fog.

When you twirl and swirl with your heart, you will be sharply aware of all beauties of the world, things that you had not noticed or given heed to when you were not dancing with your heart. With the dance within you, you will have a broader sense of acceptance of who you are, and therefore your acceptance of others and the world around you will grow and grow to the point that you are spiritually connected with the entire universe—every creation breathes into you and you into it, fusing everything into one.

You will feel awake and alert when you waltz with your heart. Once you start dancing, you will not want to stop because the feeling will be too good and too powerful to let go, and you will crave it when you stop dancing. You will feel at peace with yourself and with the world. You will feel friendly toward those who follow in your dance steps or even toward those who abandon your dance to be lured into darkness.

When you dance, you will feel alive and free and painless, even if your body shouts of old age. Your body will grow older, but your essence will stay as young as a newly blossomed flower, but only with much more wisdom and understanding. Your dance will never grow old with age; instead, it will grow younger and wiser as each day passes for you will connect with all surrounding power to recharge your own energy.

Do I dance with my heart? You bet I do! Many joints in my body have been disfigured by severe juvenile rheumatoid arthritis since infancy, yet my heart dances freely and openly with no restraint. As we dance, my heart tells me all that it sees, so my blindness miserably fails to make me trip on my own feet.
Thus crank up the music, take my hand in yours, and let us dance with our hearts!

# Chapter VIII
# Spreading the Inspiration

In mid-June, Shirley received another invitation to contribute to a book, this time from the creator of the *Wake Up...Live the Life You Love* book series for its latest installment, which, as she was told, would be the second edition of *Finding Your Life's Passion*. Some of the co-authors in this new edition would be top professionals from all around the world, including Dr. Wayne Dyer; Tony Robbins; Wyland, highly acclaimed artist of the sea and marine life; and Carla and Lou Ferrigno, the original *Incredible Hulk* and neighbor on the network television comedy show, *King of Queens*. Needless to say, Shirley would be honored to be a fellow contributor. After receiving all the necessary information, she had submitted an expanded version of *Celebrate Your Existence, for It Is Your Privilege!* by the end of the month.

She was, however, too pre-occupied with an upcoming engagement to be completely engrossed in the excitement of a new book project. She was to have her first book signing in a bookstore, and it was not just any bookstore but her local Borders Books, Music & Cafe. Over a year earlier, she had contacted the store, but the lady to whom she had spoken did not welcome her because she was self-published; it was the same kind of refusal she had received from other bookstores. When Shirley called again this year, however, it had seemed as though their managing system had changed, and the manager asked her to mail him copies of her books. That, she knew, was a great sign. After receiving the books, the manager approved her for a signing on August 12. In conjunction with her signing, Shirley would give an inspirational talk. So it was the first for many for her—first signing in a bookstore and first time giving a talk.

Shirley had been busy preparing for the signing; she had E-mailed the local newspapers the press release about her signing. As a result, a local publication, *Pulse, the Entertainment Beat*, interviewed her and published the interview with the cover of her autobiography on a full page. A reporter from *Millbrook Roundtable*, a local newspaper, E-mailed her to tell her that he would like to cover her book signing event. It appeared as though all was going to go well.

***

"There's not many people here." Juliet looked around her in Borders.

"I hope people will come," said Shirley. "I wonder how many people read the publication." *Pulse* was the only publication that had mentioned her signing. "The reporter from *Millbrook Roundtable* should be here any minute."

"*If* he's coming at all. He never wrote back to you to confirm it after you E-mailed him back."

"He didn't need to confirm it; he said that he would cover the event. I told him that I would be available from 1:30 onward."

Yet two o'clock arrived without any sign of the reporter. Shirley shrugged. Her signing had officially begun. Why let it get her down? She would enjoy her time. It was their loss, not hers.

"Hi, Erin," Juliet greeted Shirley's friend when she appeared in front of them, along with three other people: her mother; her new boyfriend, Jack; and Jack's sister.

"Erin, I'm so glad you came! Thank you all for coming. My book signing has just started, though no one is here besides you." The store had announced her signing through the loudspeaker, but it failed to bring anyone over to her table.

"There's not many people here," noticed Erin.

"Oh well. That's okay. I'm going to give my talk in a little bit." Shirley wanted to wait some more to see if anyone else would join them. Fifteen minutes passed and no one came. "Okay, so I guess I'll start then. Mom, you have the camcorder ready?"

"Yes," came Juliet's voice somewhere in front of her. "But I can't seem to get it to work. What happened?"

Jack offered to help. "The batteries appear to be dead."

"Dead? But the camcorder is new. That's terrible! I really want to tape her speech."

Shirley could hear how disappointed Juliet was. "Mom, it's okay."

"I can't believe this," muttered Juliet. "I really wanted to save it."

The group of four had an idea: Erin could fetch their camcorder from home. She lived in a neighboring town, so it would take about forty minutes for her to return to the bookstore. "She'll get it so you can record it," her mother told Juliet.

"Oh, it would be too much trouble for you," said

Juliet.

"No, it won't. Erin will be back soon."

As soon as Erin left, a kind woman whom Juliet and Shirley knew walked in with her daughter. "Wow, what a nice surprise!" exclaimed Shirley. "Thank you so much for coming!"

When Erin returned with the camcorder, Jack offered to tape Shirley's talk. On the count of three, the smiling Shirley began her talk. "Good afternoon, everyone. I'm absolutely honored and delighted that you could join me today." She had planned to thank the store manager and the staff for making the event possible, but the manager was on his break and no staff member was present.

"I'm Shirley Cheng. I'm an author and poet of five books, two of which I co-authored with highly acclaimed experts like Dr. Wayne Dyer, Jack Canfield, and John Gray, including the latest installment in the bestselling inspirational series, *Wake Up...Live the Life You Love*. Unfortunately, both books are not yet released, so I have only three books to sign today. But I will take pre-orders for them and send you the autographed copies when they are published.

"To start off my talk, 'I'm Not Disabled, I'm Ultra-Abled,' I want to give you a personal quote of mine: Although I'm blind, I can see far and wide; even though I'm disabled, I can climb high mountains. Let the ropes of hope haul you high!

"Let me share with you a bit of my life story so you may get to know me as a person not just as a writer, and my story is detailed in my autobiography, which is the book I'll be focusing on in a bit."

After Shirley told the audience her life story, she said, "So back to my autobiography: Before I became an author, my mother had always wanted someone to write a biography of my life, so when I started writing professionally, I said, 'Hey, let me write my autobiography. Who else could do a better job telling my experiences than I can?'

"I wrote my autobiography for mainly two reasons: To empower, inspire, and motivate others to go for their gold medals in life as I have, despite insurmountable challenges; to bring humor, hope, and healing, and to tell others that no matter what happens to you, no one has the power to destroy your spirit.

"And the second reason why I wrote this book is to bring awareness to others about some of the serious issues plaguing our society, specifically the two issues I'm advocating now: I'm advocating parental rights in children's medical care and aide/caregiver monitoring and screening for students with special needs or the disabled people in general.

"In America, parents risk losing custody of their children forever when they disagree with doctors' recommended treatments or even when they want a second opinion. This nightmare has happened to numerous parents throughout American history, including to my mother. She lost custody of me twice only after disagreeing with doctors recommended treatments—and those treatments would have ended my young life. The last case in 1990 made international headlines; she was on CBS *This Morning* with Paula Zahn. Why did she lose custody of me? The doctor wanted to operate on six of my joints in one operation when he didn't even have any medicine to control my inflammation. My mother wisely refused the surgery. Fortunately, she won me back both times so I didn't receive the unwanted, harmful treatments.

"And I survived mistreatment and abuse from my one-on-one aides when I attended public schools; I had aides ranging from unloving to incompetent and everything in between; I complained to my schools, they ignored my voice, and I kept on hurting. There's abuse going on everywhere, from nursing homes to hospitals. When the people who have the power to prevent or stop it don't, we arrive at a sad dead end. We must remove that dead end to stop abuse from happening. What my mother and I have experienced firsthand in these two areas are detailed in my autobiography.

"I wrote my autobiography in third-person, and it reads more like a novel than an autobiography because I've made it both entertaining and eye opening; it has villains and the good guys and the battles between these opposite forces. As the subtitle indicates—*A Young Woman's Autobiography of a 20-Year Tale of Trials & Tribulations*—this book details the trials and tribulations I, along with my mother, have gone through: the challenges of finding the treatments for my JRA, dealing with its side effects, but really, what we found to be most difficult to deal with is human nature; the lack of compassion and common sense in some people is astounding. This book, of course, covers what I shared in my introduction in detail."

Afterward, Shirley delved into the inspiration realm, where she shared her secrets of being unstoppable, or ultra-abled, as she liked to call it.

"If you say that I'm madly in love with life, that will be one hundred percent true. Call me a love-sick gal! But I ask you this: What would you have missed if your existence had never existed?

"I know I am able to laugh; I am able to weep.

Without my life, I would be able to do none of these.

"Thus, let us celebrate our existences together; let us rejoice the beauty of our treasures, and embrace all of our days! Thank you!"

The corner of the bookstore where Shirley sat became alive with loud applause. "You are a hero!" remarked Erin's mother.

"Thank you." Shirley smiled from ear to ear.

"Pearl, you were just wonderful!"

"Jack, you got it taped?" asked Shirley.

"Hmm," was his reply. Shirley did not like the sound of that. "I think it's stuck. I'm afraid it didn't get recorded. It got a bit at first, but it froze. Sorry about this."

"Oh, that's okay." Shirley thought that there was always a next time.

"But Erin can send you what we've got," said Jack.

"All right," said Shirley. She could almost feel Juliet's disappointment through her skin.

After a while, the two groups of people left, but not before signing the newsletter signup sheet Shirley had brought so people could subscribe to her newsletter; her two-hour book signing was up. She had sold only one book, but it was the memory that was most important. She felt good about speaking, and wanted to do more of it. This was a start; a good start. She would now definitely open the door to speaking engagements.

Before Juliet and Shirley packed up to leave—Juliet primarily only had to take away the poster and stand, for the bookstore had ordered all the books for her signing—a woman came up to Shirley and said, "You are so inspirational! You've had me crying there."

Shirley was not aware that she had had someone else in her audience, and that the woman was a high school teacher. "She should speak at high schools; kids would really like that," she told Juliet.

The following day, Shirley asked Juliet to buy a thank-you greeting card for the bookstore manager. She wanted to express her sincerest appreciation for his kindness and consideration. He had even invited her back to hold another book signing in the fall season. Thus, a week later, her second book signing at Borders was scheduled for October 6. This time, instead of a Saturday afternoon, the usual time they set up signings, Shirley would have it on a Friday evening. This, the manager hoped, would result in more visitors and buyers for her signing.

# Celebrate Your Existence, for It Is Your Privilege!

Do you love life unconditionally? Do you accept and cherish days that are dark and dreary rather than light filled? Does your passion for life die away when life seems to play games in which you lose?

It is easy to love life when you achieve what you desire. You embrace life when things go right. But what if life throws you stones when you least expect it? How do you feel when, at times, life seems to turn its back on you? If you suddenly lost your eyesight, would you still feel passionate and continue to see past the loss, and look into a bright future, and cherish what you had the privilege to have in the past?

I know I love life unconditionally, and the flames of my passion will never die. Yes, I am passionately, madly in love with life, and, I know, it loves me unconditionally in return. But how, you must wonder, could it love me unconditionally when it has snatched my eyesight away, leaving me to yearn for the stars I can now only wish upon?

For seventeen years, I had the honor of beholding the beauty of our world; I experienced the sheer pleasure of seeing my mother's smile alight upon her eyes; I had the delight of treating my soul to the breathtaking scenes of nature: the celestial diamonds, the green velvet that blankets our Earth, and the glistening mirrors that winter creates upon our ponds;

and now, I have lovingly tucked these photographs in my mind, and I am still able to enjoy them in my heart, from which I continue to see the world. I do not scorn life for taking away my ability to see; instead, I am grateful for having owned this power before.

When you fall in love with someone, are you falling in love with a perfect person? No, because that person does not exist. Instead, you love that person for who he or she is and how he or she makes you feel. Thus, with life, acknowledge the times you have lost and be grateful for what you have won. And unlike an imperfect lover, life will never abandon you; for better, for worse, for richer, for poorer, in sickness or in health, the sunrays will never leave your side.

Knowing this, I am passionate about being alive and returning life's love with an intensity that matches the power of fire; my heart dances whenever I am thinking about my existence.

But what is being alive, really? Being alive is having the privilege to smile, laugh, taste, and touch. It is having the ability to smell the special scent your mother carries; to run with the wind; and to dance with your heart.

Without life, how could you have known the delight of waking up to the songs of birds or dancing to the rhythms the ocean makes? How could you have seen the beautiful arch across the sky after a refreshing rain? And how could you have had the chance to taste your salty teardrop on your lips?

Your existence has given you priceless treasures—treasures of the full spectrum of emotions; the sharing of feelings; your talents, ideas, and imagination; and countless other riches of the universe. Yes, you are indeed immeasurably rich, much richer than the infinite unborn souls.

True, not all the jewels your existence has given you shine and shimmer; many of them are steep mountains you must climb and deep oceans you must swim, but these challenges and obstacles are the jewels that make you stronger. Challenges are life's vaccines: they exercise your spirit to help you withstand high winds and equip your soul with the necessary tools to battle future storms.

I have received many of these vaccines; the obstacles have left numerous scars on my body in all shapes and sizes, but these marks have made me stronger and more invincible as I wait for the next high mountain to climb. I relish the taste of victory each and every time I battle and win. If there were no challenges, how could I name myself a victor? If there were no darkness, how could the stars appear so bright?

Be thankful for the gems that sparkle; focus on the gifts your existence has bestowed upon you. Do not let any dust or dirt tarnish the value of these diamonds; the dirt itself cannot touch or harm the treasures—only you have the power to ultimately soil the gems, so handle them with grace and appreciation. For each day that passes, thank for that day and its riches. Instead of waiting for a disaster to strike to be thankful for what little is left after its devastation, love and appreciate everything and everyone right now.

I embrace my existence with my whole heart and soul, and I accept all the jewels—the bright, along with the not-so-bright—my life has granted me. I cherish my existence and everything else it encompasses, knowing that I can create more wondrous treasures by using what I have. Although I'm blind, I can see far and wide as my heart tells me all it sees; even though I'm disabled, I can climb high mountains, for my spirit soars with the wind, unafraid to face any rain and hail. In spite of all the high mountains I have had to climb, I have arrived at each and every top with a smile. I have conquered thorny jungles and fiery seas and come out with stars in my arms. I am able to achieve all this, for I count my blessings every day, knowing that there is always someone out there who is in a much worse situation than I am in, so I am thankful for what I have and who is around me.

Some souls have let their troubles veil the gems, so they have been unable to treasure the diamonds. Do not let the same misfortune happen to you. When you are given life, hold on to it tightly yet delicately; cherish what has been given to you: your privilege to enjoy dawn's first rays, your power to give words of comfort to a stranger, and your fortune to receive warm embraces after a good cry. If you allow your mishaps to cloud these treasures — or do not realize the true value of challenges — you will make your situation worse than it already is, losing every good thing you do have. And watch out for the thieves who try to belittle your gifts; they are the people who refuse to recognize the worth of life.

What would you have missed if your existence has never existed?

I know I am able to laugh; I am able to weep. Without my life, I would be able to do none of these. Thus, let us celebrate our existences together and return life's unconditional love; let us rejoice the beauty of our treasures, and embrace all of our days!

# Chapter IX
# Prevailing Maternal Love

Shirley spent August searching for local events that would welcome a motivational speaker to empower their audience. She visited local event listings on radio station Web sites. She carefully read through dozens of events, many of which were not local enough or not suited for motivational speakers. She did, however, run across a handful of events where she could hold book signings: fairs and special town days, such as Hyde Park Day, celebrated annually in her neighboring town of Hyde Park. She immediately composed E-mails to the events' organizers; she also E-mailed the county's senior citizen organization and a local Presbyterian church, asking them if they would like to have a motivational speaker at their next event or if she could hold a book signing, with some of the proceeds from her book sale going to Christian Blind Mission International.

Shirley promptly received a few replies, the first from the organizer for Hyde Park Day, indicating that she was welcome to hold a book signing next to their library sale during the festival. Hence, it was settled: Hyde Park Day on September 9 would be her next engagement. One other e-mail was from the Presbyterian church, indicating that they would get back to her about the matter.

\*\*\*

"Mom, don't go when you're so ill!" Shirley said, tearfully. Her soul was utterly torn between an ill mother and her strong desire to attend Hyde Park Day. But Juliet was so terribly ill, and Shirley did not want her to go; her mother was more important than anything anytime.

But knowing how much Shirley had been looking forward to the event—and she had been, too, because she loved seeing her daughter happy—Juliet obstinately shook her head. "We'll go."

"No, please. I don't want to go. Get some sleep." Shirley knew that Juliet had been awake all night, unable to fall asleep for even a minute, for her breathing difficulty had been overwhelming; she spent the night gasping for air. It completely broke Shirley's heart. Juliet had just gotten two hours of sleep; it was eight in the morning, just one hour before they would need to be there.

"No, let's go and get it over with. You've been waiting for this day for so long!"

Juliet was up and about, dragging her body. They were ready in half an hour, and got at the fair site just in time to set up Shirley's books. "Oh, be happy," she said when she saw Shirley's gloomy look. "I'm okay."

Shirley sighed. How could she be happy when her mother was so tired and ill? But it was nothing new; Juliet was seldom well, especially when they needed to go out. Juliet struggled each and every time Shirley had an engagement. She had poor health to start with, and that capsule had worsened her condition hundredfold. Shirley forced a smile. She might as well enjoy her time when Juliet had so painstakingly brought her there.

By and by, people dropped in where Shirley and the library folks stayed, which was in a barn-like building. Although it was steaming hot outside, the temperature inside felt just right for Shirley. Most people simply took a cursory look toward Shirley's way before heading over to the library sale of used books that cost no more than a dollar each for paperbacks. Shirley inwardly cringed at the prices of her brand-new trade paperbacks. *It is no wonder no one even wants to touch my books*, she thought; she could not help but be a bit disappointed.

By lunchtime, Juliet went out to buy some food. Minutes later, she returned with a plate of chicken and rice for both of them. It had been their first time eating out in a long while, and Shirley relished in the experience. Mother and daughter contentedly spent the time together.

"Are you sure we can go to Canada?" Shirley asked, taking a sip of the fresh fruit shake. She had received an E-mail the previous day from Sarah, a woman who had left a kind message in her blog a month earlier, inviting her to speak at an upcoming event they, Sole Vishyuns, were co-sponsoring with Canadian National Institute for the Blind. When she had first read the E-mail, she could not believe her ears. Although it was not the first time that she had received an invitation via E-mail to speak, it was the first invitation to an international event. The event organizers had not set up a date for the event, but they wanted it to be around November. As a matter of fact, they wanted Shirley to pick the date.

"Well, after you get all the information from

your research, we would be able to go."

"It's going to be mighty hard. The plane, the taxi…"

"Yes, but let's not decide, yet."

"I'm still getting some information from them. I would so love to go!"

"It would be so great if we could go. I'm so happy for you. You make me the happiest and luckiest mother ever!"

Around three, both felt that it was best to leave. Juliet was unable to hold up any longer, and Shirley was getting bored, having nothing to do. It was her first book signing where she sold not a single copy. Shirley would remember the event not for its fun aspects but of Juliet's struggles.

\*\*\*

A week after Hyde Park Day, Shirley spoke with Sarah and Sarah's friend, Cathy, about the event in Canada which they had named Celebration of Hope. "After our last meeting with CNIB, we decided that it would be best to have you come at another time, rather than cramping so many activities into one event. This way, we can entirely focus on you," explained Sarah. "*You* would be the event. Do you like the idea?"

"That sounds great!" gushed Shirley. "It really sounds great. So when would the second event take place?"

"We're thinking of sometime in February or afterward," supplied Cathy. "In the springtime, maybe."

"How about April?" suggested Shirley.

"Yes, that would be great. You know how the

winter is over here." Cathy laughed.

"What would be a good date?" asked Shirley.

"You pick the date, my dear!" said Sarah.

Shirley felt terribly honored. "Thanks! I'm really excited about the event. Thank you so much for inviting me to speak."

"No, thank *you*," said Sarah. "For the event on November 11, we'd love to show our guests a video of you. Would you be able to videotape something for us, perhaps an introduction, and share with others what you'll talk about in the next event?"

"We can help you with it if you need help," offered Cathy.

"Oh, I'd love to. No, I won't need help, thank you. I can definitely tape something. When will you need it?"

By the end of their conversation, Shirley had a new assignment due in as soon as possible in time for November 11, the date Shirley herself had picked for their event since it fell on a Saturday, a day she felt would be best for such an event. Once done with the taping, she would mail them the DVD. She would E-mail them the date for their April event. It seemed as though she was actually going to go, even though she had not given a definite answer.

# Chapter X
# Taking the Great with the Okay

Juliet dressed Shirley up in a floral dress and put her waist-length hair into a ponytail. "I hope I can sell more books this time," said Shirley as Juliet was wheeling her out the door.

"Don't worry about it, Pearl. We're there for the fun of it, not for the money. It's not like you'd have to live off it." She heaved as she pushed Shirley onto the ramp and into her van, which would take them to Borders for Shirley's second book signing.

Shirley smiled wryly. "True." But making some money while having fun would be a plus. If she did depend on it, she would be dead by now.

The drive to the bookstore took about fifteen minutes. After parking the van, Juliet got Shirley out, along with the poster and its stand. After Juliet wheeled Shirley into Borders, Juliet said, "They have only one copy of each of your books on display."

"Really? There should be seventeen books altogether. I'd have to ask them about it then." And Shirley did as soon as a saleswoman greeted her. Never did she expect the answer she would receive.

"We sold them!" was the cheerful answer.

"My books, all sold out?" repeated Shirley in disbelief. Did she hear the woman correctly?

"Yes, they're all sold out! That's great!"

At first, Shirley could not say a word; she was unable to close her mouth. "Well, good thing I brought some copies with me," She finally managed to say, giggling. She still felt dazed when Juliet situated herself at the table.

"You see, if bookstores stock your books, they will be sold," said Juliet, triumphant that she could now prove her words; she had been telling it to Shirley quite a few times.

"But they won't stock them. Too many books are published each year; they can't possibly stock them all. I'm not a celebrity, so they are not interested." But that did not mean that it was impossible to get some stores to stock her books. She had made dozens of calls to bookstores, as well as sending out hundreds of E-mails, and a couple of them did order a copy of her books. Although she made only two sales, it was better than nothing. She would try again.

Even though it was Friday evening, the store had more people than on her first signing only by a narrow margin. Shirley was not expecting anyone she knew to come, so when Erin and Jack walked in, Shirley nearly yelped with delight. "You just missed my talk," she told them. She had given the same talk, this time to a new group of people, which included two college girls and two of the store workers. Juliet was able to tape her talk with her camcorder, and hoped that she would successfully get everything on tape this time. As with last time, Shirley brought along the newsletter signup sheet, and she collected several more signatures as a result.

\*\*\*

A couple of weeks following her book signing, Shirley decided to enter in the third annual *Be the Star You Are!* writing contest with her essay, *I Hold the Power*, her personal journey of overcoming blindness at the age of seventeen. It would be wonderful if she could win twice in a row. She took only a day to write the essay, but did not submit it right away. She usually held her entry for several days to make sure it was as perfect as she could get it.

A few days later, Shirley suddenly was hit with a strong desire to write a fourth book. Although she had had such desires before, no feeling was as strong and invincible. For years, she had wanted to title a book of hers *Waking Spirit*, and it seemed as though she at last could make that dream come true, to quench that thirst. She decided that she would compile some of the pieces she had written in the past couple of years into the book. The book would not only consist of prose but poetry as well. *Now, what kind of poems should they be?* she thought, thinking of all the different kinds of poems. The idea of writing haiku, a kind of poetry she had never even considered writing, flashed into her mind like a bolt of lightning. *Why not try my hand at haiku? It seems so easy to write.* She signed onto the Internet and performed some searches on haiku. She read that haiku consists of three lines, with five syllables on the first line, seven on the second, and five on the last. The poetry should highlight animals and nature wonders, including the four seasons. *Perfect*, she thought, happily. She was a person who cherished nature and animals, so this kind of poetry would just be perfect for her to write; she would thoroughly indulge in every second while writing it. Along with haiku, she would write some freestyle poems, both rhyming and non-rhyming. She would also play around with ballads, her favorite style of poetry.

That night, she could hardly stop thinking about her new book project. As thoughts swam through her head, one thought hit her: let Cynthia Brian write a foreword for the book. She smiled as she drifted into sleep late that night, or rather that following morning, as it was in the wee hours.

Shirley began working on *Waking Spirit* first thing in the morning after checking her E-mail. She also E-mailed Cynthia to see if she would like to write the foreword. To her great joy, Cynthia replied that she would be honored to write it, and would need some information from Shirley to help her do so. In a few days, Shirley E-mailed her a pdf file containing all the necessary materials.

Within two weeks, *Waking Spirit* was completed, with 102 haiku, which took Shirley a week to write; the most she wrote in a single day was thirty-two. Before Thanksgiving Day, Cynthia E-mailed her the foreword, which Shirley felt was absolutely excellent; it easily topped her expectations. Soon thereafter, she sent her manuscript to the editor who had edited *Dance with Your Heart*. At the same time, a cover designer worked on the cover, following Shirley's meticulous directions.

In December, editing was complete. Shirley had purchased the new distribution service Lulu offered: an ISBN that registered her as the official publisher. In other words, she was now an honest-to-goodness self-publisher, unlike with her previous books. It did not matter if you did all the publishing tasks on your own, as Shirley did, you would not be the true publisher of your book if you did not own the ISBN number. But

Shirley always told others she was self-published, since Lulu primarily acted like a printer. Now she was the founder and CEO of Dance with Your Heart! Publishing, which meant that she would need a logo. Thus, she found an illustrator, who agreed to take on her logo creation project. Her logo would have a white flying dove against a large red heart as its background. Next to the picture would be the name of her publishing company in her own handwriting. It was not only unique, it was personal.

During the publishing process for *Waking Spirit*, Shirley then thought of finishing up producing her fifth book, *Parental Rights in Children's Medical Care: Where Is Our Freedom to Say No? A Look at the Injustice of the American Medical System*, her parental rights advocacy book, which she had compiled from all the material she wrote while working on her pitches to the media.

She then remembered what Margaret had said; indeed, she would have not only one but two new books in 2007.

# Chapter XI
## Twice a Winner

"Congratulations upon winning Honorable Mention in the Be the Star You Are! 3rd Annual Essay Contest," was the news that greeted Shirley on the morning of January 11, 2007.

"Mom," Shirley called, "I received Honorable Mention for my essay, *I Hold the Power*!"

"I'm so thrilled for you, Pearl!"

Shirley replied to Cynthia Brian's E-mail to express her honor and delight. "I am going to do a little boogie woogie," she wrote. "What a great way to start the New Year, again!"

She certainly had been having good luck during the Dog Year, but it would soon be replaced by the Year of the Pig, and she was going to hold a book signing during the Chinese New Year celebration just as she had the past two years. This year, the event would be on February 10 at the same high school as last year's. She would sign four books and take pre-orders for *Waking Spirit* and *Wake Up...Live the Life You Love: Finding Life's Passion* (they had decided to call it *Finding Life's Passion* instead of *Finding Your Life's Passion, Second Edition*), the book to which she had contributed her article, *Celebrate Your Existence, for It Is Your Privilege!* The book would be released in spring.

Juliet planned to take Shirley alone to the party this time. Not only was it costly to have someone stay with them, it was mostly unnecessary, even though Juliet would have difficulty pushing Shirley. Shirley insisted that they should have someone, but Juliet simply refused.

Thus, Juliet brought Shirley alone on the day of the book signing. It had been a mild winter; their first snow had fallen about ten days earlier. Normally, it would have started snowing around Thanksgiving. But on this particular February evening, it was cold to the bones. Shirley buried her face in the thick scarf around her neck, partially covering her face. She wore a wool hat tied under her chin. She was snuggled in a leather coat, but it did not feel warm enough. She kept her hands inside its sleeves. She did not like to wear mittens. "You can put more books on my lap," Shirley told Juliet. She wanted to pile as many books as she could hold, so they could get inside and stay inside without having the need to have Juliet travel out to get more books.

"Are you sure you can hold all these?" Juliet did not want to hurt Shirley's legs with the weight of the books.

"I'm fine," came the muffled reply. It was too cold to breathe. Shirley kept her face in the scarf and her hands tight on the books as Juliet rushed them inside. The books nearly slipped from her hands when the wheelchair went over a bump at the entrance. "Whew!"

*Plop!* A few books crashed onto the floor. Juliet picked them on and continued on their way. They had their table in the same spot as last time. Juliet situated Shirley behind the table and stood the poster on the stand. They were all set. Now it was up to other people to swarm in like hungry bees to buy Shirley's books.

Hey, an author could dream, right?

Shirley signed nine copies, so she sold the fewest books this year than the previous years. Even still, it was the event where she sold the most books. *I'll definitely be back next year*, she thought, when they were packed to leave for home.

***

"I think I—" A loud sneeze interrupted Shirley's words. "I have a cold," she managed to say between blowing her nose.

"I was afraid of this! You must have gotten cold outside yesterday." Juliet frowned. "I should have asked the man to come to assist us; you wouldn't have gotten cold then. You wouldn't have needed to hold all those books and wait for me to pile them on you, in the cold."

To their horror, Shirley's cold quickly turned into pneumonia a few days later. She vomited all over her computer table when she no longer could hold it in; she had spent hours and any little energy she had left on a task that had proven to be fruitless. Fortunately, her laptop did not get soiled at all. She stayed in bed and did and ate nothing. She did not even have energy to lift a finger, so her computer was left untouched for most of the day. The day before, she had had a high fever but did not think it was anything serious, and she had countersigned a foreign rights contract for the non-profit section of the Women Publishing House to publish a Vietnamese edition of *Dance with Your Heart*. The translator, Nguyen Bich Lan, a courageous survivor of muscular dystrophy, had contacted her via E-mail On New Year's Day, expressing an interest in translating her books. Shirley admired Bich, who was only seven years older than she, and felt that her invincible spirit would be perfect for translating her works, so she agreed to have her translate *Dance with Your Heart*. Shirley was informed that since it was for the non-profit section, she would not receive any royalties. Shirley assured Bich that she did not mind. "Like I've mentioned before, I don't mind at all of having my book be available through a non-profit market, especially when it can reach so many readers to bring them humor, hope, and healing; so I am definitely interested," she wrote in an E-mail.

The next day, Shirley's nausea had subsided, so she went online to check her E-mail. The E-mail with the subject "ShirleyCheng.com The Pine Plains Lions Club Dinner March 12th at 6:30 to 8:00 pm" immediately caught her attention. She hit Enter and arrowed down to the body of the E-mail. She listened with interest as JAWS read:

> Dear Ms. Cheng:
> I am the President of the Pine Plains Lions Club. I am also very proud to say the second female Lions President in the club's history. We are having a dinner with our membership on March 12th and I would like to invite you as our speaker. The Lions Club is dedicated to community service in the areas beyond hearing and sight. The Lions Club was called to service and "knighted" by Helen Keller in 1925 in one of her famous and awe-inspiring speeches. We are now facing a critical time in which we have many dedicated "seasoned" Lions who are getting on in age and very few younger folks willing to do what these unsung heroes have done and are still willing to do. As a result

everyone is tired and in need of a good shot in the arm. The shot in the arm may be you- our motivational speaker!

The letter provided contact information and asked for Shirley's prompt response. Shirley was still too weak to have the energy to be delighted, let alone to reply, so she decided that the first thing she would do when she got better was reply to the invitation. She whispered the news to Juliet. It would be her first official speaking engagement; in January, she had received an E-mail from the public relations department regarding the Victory Day celebration saying, "This year, the Committee has decided to limit the speakers to breast cancer patients or researchers," and apologizing for any inconvenience. It further said that they would keep her inspirational information packet on file for future reference. And earlier that month, she had been notified that the event in Canada for April had been canceled due to unforeseen changes at the organization.

As soon as Shirley felt the least bit better two days later, with just enough energy to write, she E-mailed the Lions Club president back: "Thank you for inviting me to speak at your dinner. I'd be absolutely honored and delighted to motivate the Lions to maintain their strength and spirit so they can continue to provide the much needed support and guidance to those who need them."

Shirley promptly received a reply to confirm the speaking engagement, and was told that they had another dinner event, a zone-meeting dinner where they would invite other local Lions Club to join them, on April 9, and that she was welcome to speak there as well. Shirley felt that the later date would give her ample time to recover from pneumonia, and told the president that she would like to speak at their April dinner instead, "for several reasons," without mentioning her illness. Thereupon, both parties agreed on April 9.

# Chapter XII
# Remembering the Courage of a Lioness

"Good evening, Lions and Lionesses. I am absolutely honored and delighted to join you." Shirley flashed everyone a wide smile. Her navy blue silky dress almost perfectly matched the background of the Lions Club banner behind her. Her heart pounded with sheer excitement as she began her speech. "I must thank President Ilene for graciously inviting me to be a part of this event. I'm most appreciative of the very warm welcome."

She pictured the rows of table in front of her, and the sixty or so people who sat there, most of whom were finishing up their dinners. She imagined the gentlemen with clean shirts and nice pairs of pants, and the ladies in their casual business attire. Juliet had a man stay with them to help push Shirley, and he was videotaping her speech from the front of the audience.

"My name is Shirley Cheng. I'm a poet, author and contributing author of twelve books, two of which I co-authored with highly acclaimed experts like Jack Canfield and John Gray, including the latest installment in the bestselling *Wake Up...Live the Life You Love* series. I'm also the creator of DanceWithYourHeart.com." Shirley wished she had a microphone. Although sound did travel well in the pavilion, she still had to use energy to speak up so people at the back could hear her. For a person who could stand up to give their speech, it would have been a totally different case. Talking while sitting down did not allow her voice to travel easily. The Lions Club president stood up every time she spoke to the audience. Many in the audience were getting up for dessert, making rustling noises, although they did their best to be quiet.

"I'd like to start off by asking you a question. Do mountains really block you? Think about this question as I share with you a bit of my life stories and some of the many mountains I have faced in my life, many of which have been seemly insurmountable to conquer.

"The first mountain I encountered was the diagnosis of severe juvenile rheumatoid arthritis at only eleven months old. I contracted this painful disease after receiving a TB skin test. Everyone was stunned that such an unfortunate thing could happen. I spent my early years in constant pain; some days, I couldn't even move a muscle; I was immobile from head to toe. So I was hospitalized for many years between America and China (my mother took me to China for six times). Once in China when I was 4, I was actually able to walk for one year while receiving effective shots combined with massage therapy. For the first time, I could run and dance with the wind." Shirley smiled wistfully. "But sadly, my walking days ended when the quality of the shots went downhill." Shirley went on talking about her experiences starting schooling for the first time at age eleven, losing her eyesight six years later, and becoming an author at twenty.

"The next high mountain I need to climb is to

get the eye surgery to hopefully restore my eyesight. Then I hope to earn multiple science doctorates from Harvard University.

"My heart tells me there's a long, rugged road ahead of me with many more mountains to climb, but I am unafraid to step on it and persist onward. Instead, my soul tingles with excitement for every minute into the future. I have so much more to achieve, to experience, to know; I have much to give, to show, to express; and only with an open heart can I achieve all that I yearn to achieve.

"Although I'm blind, I can see far and wide, as my heart tells me all it sees; even though I'm disabled, I can climb high mountains, for my spirit soars with the wind, unafraid to face any rain and hail.

"I know that my future is up to me. There are always two roads to choose from in life, the road to disability and the road to ability.

You hold the power to disable yourself or enable yourself, so which road will you choose? I have chosen to be ultra-abled. Yes, I'm not disabled, I'm ultra-abled." Loud applause broke out, so Shirley had to pause. She smiled widely.

"So what's the secret that has made me ultra-abled, you ask me? There are actually two magical ingredients, both of which I've been blessed with. The first magical ingredient is my beloved mother Juliet Cheng." Applause again interrupted Shirley. Many turned to Juliet and gave her generous smiles. A gentleman held out both of his thumbs to Juliet, nodding and smiling. When the claps died down, Shirley continued, "She is the cornerstone and light of my life; she's the foundation of my happiness, strength, and success. She has saved me numerous times from the grasp of death. If it hadn't been for her, I would not be here today. Maternal love is definitely the greatest love that has ever existed." Once more, the audience clapped, followed by a smile from Shirley.

"The second ingredient that has made me ultra-abled is simply my passion for life. Life, I feel, is simply too precious to be wasted. When you're given life, you should cherish it. I cherish my life; I value every minute. I hold on to the happy moments and don't let them pass me by. I am madly, deeply in love with life. Yes, call me a love sick gal!" Many people broke out laughing, and without failing, they applauded. Shirley smiled again. Her face almost felt stiff from smiling. "But let me ask you this: what would you have missed if your existence had never existed? I know I am able to laugh; I am able to weep. Without my life, I would be able to do none of these.

"Throughout the history of mankind, mountains have sprung out of nowhere, but for those brave souls, they have chosen the same road, the road to ability, which led to happiness, success, and self-fulfillment. Their hearts have allowed them to move forward and never quit. These heroes from all walks of life have changed the world for the better, improving and touching millions of lives in many different ways. They set a positive example to the society by their never-ending determination, everyday positive attitude and actions, and their genuine desire to do good and bring good to others.

"Heroes do not dwell on the mountains or the negativity that surrounds them; instead, they choose to move forward by focusing on the good things they do have at the present and the positive side of things; they utilize the gifts of life, and what they learned from their past and their mistakes to make the present and future a brighter place for everyone, not just themselves. Life gives everyone plenty of treasures to build on and be thankful for. True, not all treasures shine and shimmer; many of them are high mountains you must climb and deep oceans you must cross. But challenges and obstacles are the gifts that make you stronger.

"Challenges are life's vaccines: they exercise your spirit to help you withstand high winds and equip your soul with the necessary tools to battle future storms. I have received many of these vaccines; the obstacles have left numerous scars on my body in all shapes and sizes," Shirley said, holding out her disfigured hands, "but these marks have made me stronger and more invincible as I wait for the next high mountain to scale. I relish the taste of victory each and every time I battle and win. If there were no challenges, how could I name myself a victor? If there were no darkness, how could the stars appear so bright?

"So, Lions, it is up to you to maintain your mighty strength, protection, and nurturing nature to continually aid and advocate for those who need your care, strength, and protection. By uniting your power, you can move mountains. Lions, continue to live up to your name as the king of the animal kingdom to promote responsible citizenship and good government and community and national and international welfare. One purpose unites us all, and it is our duty and honor to help those who need our help. Those whose eyes are veiled need your vision to move forward; those whose ears cannot hear need your guidance to detect the sound of life.

"So stand up, unite, and roar!" The audience broke out in loud laughter, accompanied by loud applause. Shirley could not help but giggle before continuing. "The future of humanity and salvation is in your hands. No mountain should be high enough to hold you back; no wind should be strong enough to blow you down. Lions, there are roads you must take; there are stars you must reach, and with great purpose in your hearts, spread your wings wide to take the flight you are destined to take in the crusade against blindness, deafness, and the other mountains of life! Thank you."

As soon as the last word escaped Shirley's smiling lips, the room shook with thunderous applause. Juliet's assistant pushed Shirley back to her table, where her books were piled. She had requested a book signing in conjunction with her talk. "Pearl, you were just excellent!" Juliet said, her voice unsteady.

"You're crying?" Shirley was incredulous.

"Do you know that you've received a standing ovation?"

"A standing ovation?" repeated Shirley, more than thrilled.

"You did such a wonderful job," Juliet said again.

Many came up to Shirley and congratulated her on a wonderful speech. The president, who had cried during her talk, said to Shirley, "We'd like you to speak at our convention, but we'd have to have it approved by others. Would you be interested?" It was the district manager's idea. He thought her speech was excellent, echoing the thoughts of most of the crowd.

"I'd be absolutely honored and delighted to!" chirped Shirley.

By the end of the event, Shirley had sold sixteen books, but only made one dollar. Having an assistant was certainly expensive! But nevertheless, she was grateful to the man, for without him, they would not have made it. The entrance to the pavilion had a high threshold, and he had used his mighty strength to nearly lift her power wheelchair from the ground in order to push it over.

# The Value of Success

What is success? What is the kind of success that is truly of greatest value in life? To answer this, we first must find out what Jehovah God wants from us. What He desires from us is what makes us truly successful.

What does God wish of us? First, let us think about what was His intent and purpose of creating us in the first place. The Bible, His holy words, clearly indicates that He created the world and humans so we can be fruitful and multiply and create a beautiful world, filled with loving, caring, honest, sincere, and trustworthy people. Knowing this, we can see that it is our core values that God cherishes, and, in turn, wishes His human creations to establish and pass on for eternity.

Thus, what constitutes a successful person is a successful human being. It is not about being a successful businessman, a successful doctor, or a successful teacher--that all comes later. Success is successfully realizing, establishing, and holding tightly to the priceless values of life.

A blue-collar man who constantly provides love and care for his elderly mother is hundredfold more successful than a billionaire who loves only his money. A mother who stands by her disabled daughter's side as opposed to a mother who appreciates only a healthy daughter displays the kind of success that is multiplied by countless times.

If you are a parent, would you love your child all the same, no matter how beautiful or ugly, how rich or poor, how smart or stupid, and how healthy or ill? If yes, then you would be a successful parent.

Are you successful when, no matter how hard you have worked and done your best, you still have not achieved your intended goal, but you have learned many valuable lessons along your journey? Yes, you are successful, and for two reasons: First, you have worked your hardest and have tried your best--the best is all we could ask from anyone. And second, you have been wise enough to learn lessons during your travel. Achieving a goal, without learning much from the process, does not make a person truly successful.

Once you have become a successful human being, you can then become a truly successful businessman, a successful doctor, or a successful teacher. If you do not have good values to start with, what would you have to expand on? A businessman who cheats money from his clients to become a millionaire is not successful. On the other hand, a man with integrity has that value from which to build his business. From there, he can become a successful businessman who will earn only honest money and attract loyal customers.

Thus, success is calculated by the spiritual values you can provide to others that can not be physically measured, not by the amount of money or the level of prestige you achieve. God does not care how much money you make or how much you donate to Him; He cares how much love you provide His other creations; that will show Him how much of His unconditional love you can return and how much faith you have in Jesus Christ. This is how He measures success, and this is how we should measure success.

I find my mother is the most successful person I

have ever known, and one of the most successful people who has ever lived. It is true that she has made many mistakes, but she has learned lessons, has done her utmost to be a most wonderful mother and person, and sets an excellent example for others of what being successful is really all about in life. I have truly learned a lot from her, and the lessons learned can lead me on my own road to great success.

# Chapter XIII
# Seizing Opportunities, Taking Chances

In mid-April, A strong nor'easter swept across New England and New York, making its way from Texas, Kansas, and Florida where it had spun at least one tornado. Central Park in Manhattan received a record-breaking amount of rain. Many roads were closed as flooding occurred; there were household items and appliances floating away. Hundreds of flights in New York were canceled. Shirley had scheduled a speaking engagement and book signing on April 15 for a bookstore's grand opening in New York City, but she had to postpone it.

"...the powerful nor'easter completely washed away my plans...I am so glad that I postponed my engagement; I'd rather be safe than sorry. Who knows what could have happened if we drove down to the city? My area got hit pretty badly. There were areas, like the soccer fields, under five feet of water. Many roads and homes were flooded, and there were mandatory evacuations. Fortunately for us, we are all safe! I also missed a book party in the city because of the weather," Shirley wrote in the May issue of her newsletter, which she had renamed *Inspiration from a Blind*. She had been sending it out monthly to her growing subscriber base. Besides just announcing her book-related news, she now included words of inspiration at the beginning of each issue in the form of short articles. She thought that, one of these days, she would write her sixth book based on her newsletter; it would make a nice self-empowerment book.

She sent out each newsletter issue on the first of the month. She usually wrote her newsletter two weeks prior to its release, so she had more news to add in the May issue about a week before sending it. This is what greeted her on the afternoon of April 25 in her inbox:

> Dear Shirley:
>
> Congratulations!
>
> Your title "*Waking Spirit: Prose & Poems the Spirit Sings* by Shirley Cheng" has placed as a "Finalist" in the "New Age Non-Fiction" category.

Shirley read the E-mail three times, then a fourth time. JAWS would not play a trick on her, right? She could hardly contain her joy. Her first book award ever! She did a little dance on her bed and jumped a few times. She had sent advanced reading copies of *Waking Spirit* to the 2007 Indie Excellence Book Awards, mentally kissing the package for good luck. The book was not yet published and it had already brought in an award. She would officially release it in early May. Juliet was out grocery shopping, so she had to wait for her to get home to share the grand news.

Shirley's mind was reeling. Not only did she have to digest the news of winning a book award but had to let the fact that she and Juliet would actually travel to Las Vegas sink in. Yes, flying on the plane—

something they had not done for thirteen years—all the way across the country. She still remembered the day she agreed to Juliet's urge...

"You must be crazy!" Shirley had almost shouted. "Flying to Las Vegas? Not just to Las Vegas, but flying on a plane? You know how difficult that would be!" Shirley knew she would sound pessimistic to many, but she was simply concerned for her mother's health. Of a certainty, she truly wanted to board the plane to the entertainment city, but she had to be realistic. With her mother's poor health, the trip could potentially damage her health further. How could she get on and off the plane, the taxi, the— "It's impossible! Forget about it."

"It's *possible*," Juliet corrected. "I can do it. I know it'll be very hard. If we can't do it, we can just turn around." She finished with a loud gasp for air.

"See, your breathing difficulty! What if you have problems breathing on the plane?"

"I'll be okay. We should make arrangements right now." She explained that they would have a man go with them to help them with everything.

Shirley thought that her mother sounded as though she had already made the decision to go. She thought for a moment, and before her mind could protest further, she said, "Okay, we'll go." She thought of the engagement in Canada that she had quite readily accepted, but she knew why: Sarah and Cathy had told her that they would accommodate her special requirements, including having people available to carry her and providing a commode and extra pillows and bed sheets in her hotel room. Compared with that, this trip to Las Vegas would be much more difficult. "Yes, we have to make the arrangements right now. I'll have to call them to book a room at the hotel. I hope it's not full." It was April 20, just twenty days before the event on May 10 at the Palms Casino Resort. It was the world premiere of *Pass It On*, an inspirational film that was said to be more promising than the famous *The Secret* film. The movie's story is by Greg S. Reid and Scott Evans, and it is produced by David M. Corbin and directed by twenty-four-year-old Jon Dixon. A handful of the world's top experts and authors, including Bill Bartmann, America's twenty-fifth richest man; David Dean; LuAn Mitchell-Halter; Brian Tracy; and Mark Victor Hansen, the co-creator of the *Chicken Soup for the Soul* book series, had starred in the movie and were scheduled to appear for the premiere and the red-carpet celebrity arrival. Robin Leach, the host of the *Lifestyles of the Rich and Famous* television show, would be the announcer for the red-carpet event. And at that event, the *Wake Up...Live the Life You Love* team would have a film shooting for some of Shirley's fellow co-authors for their own inspirational documentary. It would be Shirley's only chance to be in the film. If she missed going, she would miss a great opportunity. So for the sake of the film shooting, she had decided to go; celebrities never interested her much, so if it had been only for the premiere, she would not have agreed.

Shirley made a call to reserve a room at the Palms, but was told that it was booked for those days. Somewhat down, she hung up. Moments later, she received an E-mail, telling her that someone for the premiere had just canceled a room, so Shirley immediately called them back and booked the room. She had to laugh. "We're so lucky! Now I'll need to do some research on the post-9/11 airport regulations." She ended up spending hours researching and found the telephone number of the office that assisted people at the John F. Kennedy International Airport. After she read everything, she repeated all her findings to Juliet, doing her best not to miss a single detail. She explained about the 3-1-1 rule, where each plane passenger was allowed only one one-quart of Ziplock bag containing a three-ounce container for every liquid or gel. "They do not say if it's fluid ounces or what. But just to be safe, we'll just bring a bit of what we need," thought Shirley aloud.

Next, Juliet bought their roundtrip plane tickets. They were all set to go, alone. Juliet asked a gentleman if he could go with them to Las Vegas. "Are you kidding?" He had burst out laughing, then told her that he would get back to them, but they never heard back from him.

"The more I think about it, the more I think I can go alone," said Juliet.

"Are you sure you can do it?" Concern returned in Shirley's voice.

"We'll make it. If both airports could assist us with everything, like carrying you and calling the cabs, then we'd be fine."

Departure from New York: May 9, 2007
Arrival at New York: May 11, 2007

"Las Vegas, here we come!" Shirley giggled.

# Chapter XIV
## Flying with Faith

Outside their window, the chirps of birds became steadily audible, yet they were still quite faint and would not be noticed if one did not listen carefully. One pair of ears did listen carefully; Shirley guessed it was 3:30, the usual time when the first tweeter began. As the minutes passed, their songs crescendoed. Shirley sighed. *Might as well get up with the birds*, she thought, *since we're not making any progress here*. She was supposed to be filled with immeasurable excitement, but tiredness took its place instead.

Juliet returned her sigh. She had not slept at all, whereas Shirley had had only an hour of sleep. Not very flattering, indeed. "This is how it was every time when we had to travel on the plane. I could never sleep the entire time on our six trips to and from China."

"Are you going to be okay?"

"Are *you* going to be okay?"

"I'll be fine. Want to get up?" It was four o'clock, four hours before the taxi was to pick them up.

"Yes, let's get up and get ready." Juliet slowly got out of bed and began the preparation. She had packed almost everything in the carry-on they were bringing, except for Shirley's evening gown. It was much too delicate to be packed in the bag for long, so they had decided to add it to the carry-on on the last day.

"I will need to use the commode soon," Shirley told Juliet. She had forced down a bowl of canned black beans the previous afternoon. She wanted to make sure that she would go before they were to leave for the airport. If she did not, she would not have any place to go. She often controlled her bathroom schedule for any event this way. Eating beans was the best way; they always guaranteed timing success. But it usually had the side effect of bloating. She hoped that she would not feel bloated this time.

By eight, the sleepy pair had everything ready and waited for the cab by the door. It was already quite warm, but Shirley still wore her black jacket. "I'll give the driver a call. It's already 8:10." Juliet dialed the number from memory. The driver told them that he would be there shortly. Juliet called him again when it seemed that "shortly" had been due.

Five minutes later, Juliet announced, "He's here! Okay, we're leaving."

Shirley felt the excitement throughout her body, mind, and spirit. They were really going. This was not an exciting dream but real.

The driver carried Shirley onto the back seat of his vehicle, which to both Juliet and Shirley's pleasant surprise, was a mini van, so it would be much comfortable for Shirley to ride in. He put her wheelchair, which Juliet had rented, in the trunk. Juliet had ordered a custom-made manual wheelchair for Shirley so she no longer had to struggle with the power wheelchair. They had just received the new wheelchair, but it had a problem with its arms, so Juliet took the rented wheelchair instead.

Mother and daughter smiled at each other when the van started. Shirley broke out in giggles. She was still having a hard time believing it was for real. The van turned around in the driveway and down the small hill, and went on its way to bring them to a new adventure.

"Get some sleep," Juliet said, patting Shirley's head.

"I'll try." Shirley doubt that she could. She closed her eyes. *Good thing I don't have allergies*, she thought.

*Achoo!*

She thought too soon. She sneezed twice before blowing her nose. She had a brand-new box of tissue, and she hoped it could last. She had year-round allergies, some days so severe that she had to use an entire box of tissue in one single day. Their Jet Blue flight was at 12:45 in the afternoon. It would take about five and a half hours to arrive at McCarran International Airport. Juliet had made several calls, and the airports had assured her that assistance would be available.

Around ten, the van stopped in front of the departure building of JFK International Airport. The driver carried Shirley onto her wheelchair, got their stuff out, and bade them a good trip before driving away. He was to pick them up when they returned.

Juliet looked around the airport, trying to locate the office that assisted people with special needs. "I'd have to give them a call. Now where is the cell phone?" She rummaged in her purse but could not find it. Then she unzipped the carry-on, which Shirley held in her lap. It was surprisingly heavy for only necessities. Juliet brought only a few of her outfits and everything else belonged to Shirley.

Juliet sighed in frustration. "Where is it?" She

took out one item after another until Shirley was covered with them. Her evening gown was tossed unceremoniously.

"Ah, it's right here!" Juliet at last found it, in an easy-to-locate area of the carry-on bag.

*That's what lack of sleep does to you*, thought Shirley, hidden under her gown.

"Yes, we need some help here. We're right at the departure building," Juliet shouted into her cellular phone above all the noise around them. "No, we don't need a wheelchair. We need help to go through security and board the plane."

Yet all the trouble had been pointless, because it turned out that the man who had been standing right by them could help. Juliet dumped all the contents back into the carry-on and stuffed Shirley's evening gown inside. She followed the man, who pushed Shirley toward the checking area.

"All liquids out," he told Juliet, who took out the two Ziplock bags, containing the few liquids they brought. They did not bring any toothpaste, for Shirley had learned that the hotel provided them.

"Shoes off," Juliet was further told when she got in line for security.

"Shoes off! My…" Juliet was saying.

"My, things have changed," Shirley finished her thought. They pushed her to a different line, where a woman gently felt her hair, body, and shoes with her bare hands. She used a hand-held detector to check her wheelchair. She also unzipped the small bag that was tied to her wheelchair; it counted as her purse. Even her box of tissue went under scrutiny.

"Okay, everything's finally done," said Juliet, returning to Shirley's side. "You okay?"

Shirley nodded in reply. "Where do we wait?"

Juliet pushed her to the waiting area just by the security checkpoint. "Right here."

They had two hours of waiting to do.

"You don't look too well!" Juliet touched Shirley's forehead.

"I'm okay, it's just that my nose is bothering me." Shirley blew her nose. "I hope the Earplanes will work." The last few times she was on planes, her ears hurt her tremendously. While Shirley was researching for their trip, she had come across products called Earplanes that could prevent ear pain. "I sure hope they'll work, or else my ears would be in agony now that I have allergies."

"Do you want something to eat?"

Shirley shook her head. "You should eat something."

"I ate late last night, so it's still keeping me full." But moments later, Juliet was tempted to buy a turkey sandwich, hoping that it would not make her ill. She finished it in time for their flight.

The loudspeaker announced that boarding would start for their flight number shortly. Juliet jumped to her feet. She went to the counter, where she already had been twice, asking for assistance, but they only ignored her. "Can't you see that we need help? She needs to board the plane first."

A man pushed a wheelchair to her in response. "No, we don't need a wheelchair. We need help boarding the plane. My daughter is on the wheelchair and we need someone to carry her." Juliet's voice rose in frustration.

At last, they told her that they could board the plane, so she promptly pushed Shirley through the connecting hall and onto the plane. There was still one thing that needed to be done: to carry Shirley. No one volunteered.

"Ma'am, I can't carry her," a crew member on the plane told Juliet. "I'm a man."

"But we need a man to carry her."

"I really can't," he protested further. "I'm a man."

"She's just a little girl!"

Shirley did not know whether to laugh or cry. She rolled her eyes instead. *This is absolutely absurd*, she thought. Someone had to carry her if they wanted to take off.

Finally, a male passenger volunteered to carry Shirley onto her seat in the front row, reserved for children or special-needs people. "Thank you so much," Juliet said. "I'll help you in a two-man lift. Please watch her feet and legs. She has severe arthritis." They carefully carried the petite Shirley onto her seat.

Around two, the plane took off to the Desert City. For the very first time, Shirley asked God for a safe takeoff, flight, and landing.

# Chapter XV
## Pushing Forward

"We thank you for traveling on Jet Blue…" The loudspeaker confirmed a safe landing at McCarran International Airport.

"We're here!" Even until now, Shirley was still stunned they had come. She asked Juliet to take out the Earplanes from her ears. "They worked like a miracle. My ears didn't hurt a bit!" She felt the box of tissue and discovered she had used half of it already. She had been sneezing during the entire flight, and stopped only just before landing. She leaned forward in her seat. She felt stiff all over; it had been an uncomfortable ride because the seats were tilted backward, hurting her legs. She gritted her teeth when pain shot up from her knees as she moved them. She had been changing position in her seat, but apparently it had not helped. "I need to move my legs around, so I can be carried." But in her position, she was unable to move them enough to loosen the stiffness. She would just have to endure the inevitable pain that would come during the lift.

They would deplane last, so it would work out for everyone. They had a gentleman to carry Shirley onto her wheelchair and help them out of the airport. He pushed Shirley onto a train inside the airport that would bring them to the other terminal, where they could exit the building.

"Fortunately you are here to help us," said

Juliet. "Or else, I wouldn't have known where to go." She had never heard of this kind of train service. Terminals were so confusing to her.

"Your first time here?"

"Yes!"

"Where are you from?"

"New York. It's so..."

"It's so different here, huh?" Then he turned to Shirley. "You're here for partying."

Shirley giggled. And she would have a ball!

When they got outside, he and the driver of a mini van, or a handy-bun as they called it, carried Shirley onto the front passenger's seat. Juliet put the seat belt around her.

The drive to the hotel took less than ten minutes. Juliet oo-ed and ah-ed along the entire way. The city was very different than New York City; it had wide roads and casinos everywhere, and palm trees dotted the sidewalks. The traffic was not congested; all vehicles could travel with relative freedom.

The driver carried Shirley back to her wheelchair alone, and told Juliet that she could call them up when they returned to the airport. With everything ready, Juliet pushed Shirley into the casino hotel. "Goodness," she said when she saw all the slot machines. The lobby was literally filled with them, flashing and beeping.

At the front desk, Juliet requested, "Please bring six pillows and sixteen, no, eighteen bed sheets." They had brought Shirley's own pillows and bed sheets when they attended the last event in New York City, for Shirley could sleep comfortably with her pillows (the pillow on which she laid her head was thin, a kind that seemed impossible to find now); this time, it was impossible to bring them on the plane. "My daughter needs them to support her arms and legs." The woman told her that they would send a maid up and that Juliet could ask for the items then.

The exhausted pair, after traveling about twelve hours, released sighs when their bodies touched the soft beds. But it was not yet time to rest for Juliet; she had to make sure Shirley had something to eat first.

"No, Mom, I am too tired, and I will go to bed now. You go ahead and order room service. I am simply too tired." Shirley could hardly keep her eyes open. "You must get some rest."

"You don't want to eat anything?"

Shirley just shook her head. She had no more energy left to speak. Even though she had stopped sneezing, her chest was starting to feel tight. She had chronic bronchitis and asthma, which could act up when her allergies were severe. Yet, she kept her discomfort to herself; she knew that Juliet was exhausted, so she did not want to add more work and worry upon her heart. She hoped that it would go away by itself as she slept. It was quite uncomfortable, but it did not get to the point that she was gasping.

***

"Mom," came Shirley's quiet voice the following morning. She really hated to have to tell her mother, but she had no other choice. Plus, her film shooting session was scheduled for 2:30 that afternoon, so she had to be well and look well for the shooting, and to have energy to last the entire day, so she reluctantly said, "Please do not worry, but I need to use the asthmatic medicine." She braced for a loud gasp. Sure enough, it came, quite loudly, too.

"You're having an asthma attack?"

"I'm okay, I just feel very tight. Just call the front desk and ask for an oxygen tank. They should have them."

"I was so afraid of this! Okay, I'll call now." Juliet's finger trembled as she dialed the front desk. "My daughter has asthma and she needs to use oxygen. I have the medicine; we just need an oxygen tank, so I can use it for her." To both of their relief, the operator told her that she would send in security right away.

Minutes later, a few quick knocks sounded on their door. Juliet rushed to it and opened the door to three men, who pushed in an oxygen tank.

Shirley was in her bed, dressed in her aqua nightgown. She had not been up, and her hair was tangled. But who cared at this time?

Juliet immediately prepared the medicine, and once completed, gave the oxygen mouthpiece to Shirley, who readily took it in her hand.

After a few minutes of treatment, Shirley nodded at Juliet, her eyes smiling. Juliet exclaimed, "She's much better!" By the time the treatment was complete, Shirley's chest felt fully relieved.

"We're glad to help. If you need anything else, just call us," one of the security men said before they left. "Enjoy your stay here."

Juliet turned to her daughter after closing the door. "You are all better?"

"Yes! It's so fortunate that we brought my medicine." Everywhere they went, Juliet never failed to bring some with them. Shirley developed asthma at age fourteen after a couple cases of back and forth pneumonia; she became seriously ill because the one-on-one aides she had to help her in school did not dress her up well during winter, and one had even come to school very ill, giving Shirley her illness.

Juliet ordered a bowl of Cream of Wheat for Shirley, who did not have much appetite, but she decided to try it before they set out for their big day.

Around eleven, Shirley frowned. She felt that she needed to go to the bathroom. She had not eaten anything the previous day, so she was more than annoyed when she still had to go. She had planned not to go. *Must be the leftover beans*, she thought with distaste. How was she going to get on the toilet? There was no way Juliet could carry her, let alone so many times—from the bed to the wheelchair, from the wheelchair to the toilet, then back to the wheelchair and lastly to the bed. If they had a commode, it could be placed next to the bed, so Juliet would need to carry Shirley only twice, but even that was two times too many. So she hesitated, thinking that she might be able to hold it in. To her dismay, she realized she could not hold it in. If she was successfully in holding it in, she would not have the full energy required to be her best.

For the second time that morning, Shirley had to reluctantly tell her mother something undesirable. "I have to go to the bathroom. Mom, you must call security to carry me onto the toilet." She hoped that Juliet would not protest, but she did anyway.

"I can do it."

"You're crazy! Your hands would fall off!" Shirley was not exaggerating. Juliet's hands were much worse than they had been when they attended BookExpo America 2005. Her hands were severely damaged from both all the chores and her car accident, but more so because of how she overworked herself around the house. For a healthy person, hours upon hours of household chores would not cause such damages to their hands, but "healthy" had never been a word to describe Juliet. Her hands were numb, painful, and swollen. She had a severe case of carpal tunnel syndrome; post-accident nerve damage; and painful tendons. Now, she could not even feed herself or hold a piece of paper without experiencing much pain. At times, she was in pain even when she was not doing anything. How could she possibly carry Shirley even once, let alone four times?

"You won't be able to go comfortably if people come. We don't know how long you'd have to wait."

"I'll be fine! Please call them."

"No, I can do it."

Shirley knew she was not going to win, so she let Juliet carry her when she was ready to go. "Ouch!" Shirley was not used to having Juliet carry her since she had not been carried in this unique way for quite some time: with Juliet's hand under her left leg and the other arm around her back. It had been a comfortable way for both of them when Juliet was able to carry her on a daily basis. Juliet struggled as she put Shirley on her wheelchair. Shirley heard her panting loudly. She must be hurting overwhelmingly, Shirley knew.

Juliet still had to carry her onto the toilet. "Ready?" She was still panting.

"You'd better call security! You can't carry me again!" Shirley's voice rose.

Juliet simply hushed her, then lifted her off the wheelchair.

"Ah!" Shirley gasped. Juliet had almost dropped her; she quickly put Shirley back on the wheelchair to prevent an actual fall.

After another lift, Juliet got her on the toilet. Both of them sweated and panted.

"You must call the security men when I'm done."

"Yes, I'd have to. Now, go."

"Okay, pull my pants back up and call them," said Shirley after she was done.

"You went okay?"

Shirley nodded. "Flush the toilet, too."

After Juliet wiped her, pulled her pants on, and flushed the toilet, she called security. She would not be able to lift Shirley again even if both of their lives depended on it.

Minutes later, just as Shirley's behind was getting painfully numb, the security men knocked on their door. Juliet opened the door to the same men who were there earlier with the oxygen tank. First, they had seen her in her nightgown, her hair tangled; now, they had to rescue her from the toilet. Not the least bit flattering, but certainly memorable. They carried Shirley onto the wheelchair, then onto the bed.

"If you need anything else, just let me know," was their kind offer before they left.

Shirley sighed and Juliet laughed; Shirley soon joined in the laughter. "They must be wondering why we are here in the first place," Juliet managed to say between giggles.

"They'd never guess that I'll be in a film; every time, everyone always thought you were the one who was on the business trip, just bringing your little daughter along." Most had thought Shirley was still a high school student. She took a deep breath, trying to stop laughing, and continued, "What time is it?"

"It's 12:30."

"Okay, time to get ready! I could hardly wait! What a long and fun day it will be." The day had not started out dully, either, to say the least.

When both of them had finished dressing to look their best, though most time was spent with Juliet making Shirley to look her best, it was already two. Juliet called security to help her carry Shirley onto her wheelchair. The men that came this time were not the same men as prior times. "Too bad they didn't see me in my best!" Shirley laughed, smoothing down her evening gown. "Guess they'll always remember me sitting on the toilet."

"You look like a mermaid, very beautiful, a natural beauty!" commented Juliet, admiring Shirley in the blue shimmering gown. "It's just like an ocean." Different shades of blue and green made it look as though Shirley was wearing the colorful ocean world.

By 2:22, both ladies were in the main lobby, where they were to meet the media personnel for the *Wake Up...Live the Life You Love* team. Shirley had called the woman on her cellular phone earlier, and they had scheduled to meet at the main lobby.

"Is this Shirley?" a woman with a southern accent asked Shirley a minute later.

"Hi, Nancy, it's a pleasure to meet you!" Shirley took out her hand, which Nancy warmly shook.

"You look absolutely beautiful! What a beautiful dress!"

"Thank you!"

"They are still upstairs in the room; they will come down for your shooting. Let's see if we can have the shooting at the back of the restaurant, away from all the noise." Nancy led them to a restaurant inside the hotel. Shirley felt it was quite chilly, and hoped that they would find another place for the shooting. To her delight, Nancy soon said, "Let's go upstairs to have your shooting in the room, where it will be nice and quiet." So up the elevator they went.

"It's a pleasure to meet you," Shirley greeted Larry, shaking his hand, when they went inside the room.

"You look very nice," he said.

"What a great color," remarked the film director. "So you're all ready?"

"Yes," Shirley said, almost breathlessly. She was too excited for words. She knew exactly what she was going to say in the film. She did not know how long it could be—no one told her when she asked—so she thought that keeping it around ten minutes would be fine. "So I can start now?"

"Whenever you're ready. It's filming now," the director replied.

"Hi, my name is Shirley Cheng. I'm a motivational speaker, advocate, poet, author of five books and contributing author of eight books..." was how Shirley began. "Do mountains really block you or can you actually create a valley of gold from them? I know I have turned my mountains into heaps of gold, though many of the mountains have been seemly insurmountable to conquer. Soon after my birth in 1983, I faced my first mountain..."

About ten minutes into the shooting, Shirley finished it with, "Let us all dance with our hearts to the music of life!"

"That's just phenomenal!" exclaimed the director. "I think that's fabulous."

"That was really good," said Larry.

"Thank you." Shirley could not stop grinning from ear to ear.

"Pearl, you were just unbelievable!" Juliet gushed. She had been stock still during the filming and was completely mesmerized by her daughter. She was so darn proud to be her mother.

"Although it was great, I'd like to have something from which to choose; I may use both parts. I'd like to film an interview of you and Larry, instead of just having the monologue," the director explained. "Would you like to do an interview?"

"Yes, I'd love to," Shirley answered.

The interview went smoothly, and lasted less than ten minutes, Shirley guessed. "That's just great, too. Thank you for letting me have something to choose from," the director said before it was time for everyone to leave; the filming crew would be filming downstairs next.

Back in the lobby, Juliet exclaimed more to Shirley; she had not had the freedom to do so loudly and frequently in the room. "You were too, too good!"

"I'm glad it went well. So what time is it now?"

Juliet checked her watch. "It's only three. Where should we go now? Is it time for the red-carpet arrival?"

"No, that won't be until eight. We have to get our tickets, but that won't be open till five."

"So we have time to take some photos!" Juliet loved taking photographs of Shirley.

"And some videotaping, too," Shirley pointed out. They had brought their camcorder.

"Let's go out. I want to film you outside in front of the hotel. You won't be cold?"

"No way." Shirley had checked the Las Vegas

forecast before their trip, and all days were said to be in the high nineties. "I'll be hot."

Once outside, Shirley remarked, "It doesn't feel that hot at all." It must be the humidity in New York that had made it feel so much warmer than Las Vegas, even when the temperatures were only in the seventies. Shirley took a deep breath of the fresh air. *So this is what Vegas is like*, she thought, smiling a contented smile. No, even until now, she could not believe they were there. Perhaps, after the dream was over, she could.

# Chapter XVI
# Wheeling on the Red Carpet

"There's Bill Bartmann," Juliet whispered to Shirley, "right in front of us." It was after five; they had received their tickets, and now they were inside the Brenden Theatres, where the premiere of *Pass It On* was scheduled, and by the sound and feel of it, Shirley guessed that it was the press junket. Shirley detected flashing lights all around her, and Juliet told her that they were the press snapping shots of the top experts, who introduced themselves one by one in front of them. "He has such kind eyes," Juliet said, referring to Bill.

"I'd want to take a photo with him," Shirley whispered back.

"Yes, I'll ask him once I get a chance."

Many people filed out after the press junket. "What's next?" Juliet asked Shirley.

"I'm not sure. The junket was not in the schedule I have. Just follow the crowd, I suppose." They learned that it was time for a casual party; many had simply gathered around the food court.

"Let's get something to eat," suggested Juliet.

"You go ahead; I don't want anything," came the usual answer from Shirley.

"You don't want anything?" came the usual exclamation from Juliet.

"No."

Juliet urged Shirley further to no avail. "Then I'm not going to eat anything. I was going there to get food just for you."

"Let's just wait here for the red-carpet celebrity arrival to start."

An hour later, Juliet laughed. "I saw Robin Leach! He's there getting ready to make the announcements, it seems. I recognized him right away." Juliet had watched his show years ago; Shirley never had, since she never cared much about celebrities and their extravagant lifestyles. When she had her eyesight, the only television shows she ever watched were animal and science shows on Animal Planet, Discovery Channel, and TLC, along with *I Love Lucy*, *Unsolved Mysteries*, a few game shows, and the news. Her classmates had had good reasons for calling her a nerd, which she actually secretly relished. They always saw her nose buried in a book.

"I'd like to take a photo with him, too," said Shirley. "I want to take photos with them all."

"Yes, I'll call each one over when I can."

"Give me my book." Shirley wanted to hold the hardback of *Waking Spirit* they brought. Juliet handed her the book, on which a gold seal boldly exhibited Shirley's Indie Excellence award. It was officially published. From the small bag tied to her wheelchair, Shirley got out a small pile of her business cards, which were newly printed and had a completely new design from her first batch; they listed Shirley as an author, poet, motivational speaker, self-empowerment expert, publisher, and advocate, all in bold letters, under her name, which was the largest print on the card. The card also displayed her logo. She planned to give out her card to anyone who spoke to her. She was here, after all their hard work, so why not use it to her full advantage? Why not make the most of their trip?

Getting out their camcorder from the same bag that held *Waking Spirit*, Juliet told Shirley, "I'm going to videotape the place." While she was videotaping Shirley and her surroundings, Shirley thought she heard a man calling her. She turned her head in the direction of the source of the voice.

"Hi, Shirley, I'm Ron, the senior editor for *Wake Up...Live the Life You Love*. It's a pleasure meeting you."

"Oh, really?" Shirley immediately held out her hand. "It's great to finally meet you, Ron!"

"It's a pleasure meeting you, too. I heard how great a job you did during the taping. Everyone's talking about it."

Shirley could not help but laugh. "Thank you!"

Juliet stopped her camcorder and came over to where the two were. "You know her?" she asked Ron.

"Yes, I'm the senior editor..." Much of what he said was drowned out by the commotion.

Shirley told her, "He's the senior editor of the book series."

"Oh!" It was clear that Juliet was pleased to meet him as well.

Before he left, he told them how her story contribution was appreciated and how well they thought of her.

Shirley's attention was returned to the red-carpet arrival when she heard Robin's voice. She could not help but giggle hearing Robin's British accent. She could never get tired of listening to the accent. Juliet sometimes mimicked their accents, making her laugh unfailingly. She listened as Robin announced and introduced each top experts. Some of the experts, including Brian Tracy and Denis Waitley, could not make it to the event, certainly not to anyone's surprise but greatly to their disappointment.

"Is there a red carpet?" Shirley asked, trying to make out the color of the flooring to no avail. She could faintly see colors only when the objects were close to her, and the objects either had to be relatively large or own a bold or bright color.

"There's actually no red carpet," replied Juliet.

"They ought to have one." Shirley loved red carpets; they always made places look regal no matter where they were.

During the red-carpet arrival, Juliet snapped a few photographs of Shirley. As she was taking another photograph, a gentleman came over to them and bent down next to Shirley, so Juliet could take a picture of them.

Not knowing who he was, Shirley simply thanked him and handed him a business card. She was surprised when the gentleman kissed her hand before leaving.

"That was someone I had wanted to ask for a photo with!" Juliet was pleasantly surprised that she did not even have to ask. She did not know who he was, but felt that he looked kind. She would check the photographs on the *Pass It On* Web site when they returned home to see who he was. Shirley had showed her the Web site, so that was how she recognized Bill Bartmann.

"Okay, I'm going to ask Robin now." Juliet wove through the crowd and made her way to his side. He told her that he would be with them shortly, as he still needed to make more announcements.

Moments later, as he was passing through the

crowd, he was stopped several times. Juliet went to his side again, and he said, "I never forget things." He walked over to Shirley and posed for the shot as Juliet clicked her camera.

By the end of the red-carpet arrival, Shirley had taken photographs with a handful of well-known personalities. She still had not gotten a chance to take one with Bill.

Next on the schedule: *Pass It On* world premiere. The theatres were packed over their maximum capacity; several unlucky souls had no seats. One such unlucky soul was Juliet. No one around them would offer their seat, so Juliet ended up sitting on the hard edge of someone else's seat; the raised edge was painful to sit on and it was cutting into her behind, but Juliet had no choice but to grit her teeth and wait for the film to be over. She refused to sit on the floor when Shirley suggested that. Little did she know that the painful seating situation would cause her a few weeks of infection.

During the film, Juliet quietly said, "You know, they are talking about everything you've written!"

"I was just thinking of the same thing." Shirley received surprise after surprise as the minutes passed. She felt as though they had made the film based on her own writing. What did that mean? It meant that what Shirley had been writing matched what the world's top leaders were teaching others—in other words her own content was among the best of the best.

The film was over in about two hours, and everyone filed out of the theatres. But the day was not over yet: they had a cocktail party to attend at the hotel's nightclubs, the Moon and Playboy Clubs. Juliet, now with a sore behind, pushed Shirley out of the theatres, following the crowd.

"Have a great evening, you beautiful women!" a female voice called out to them.

"No, you are beautiful," said Juliet, giggling.

Shirley learned that the kind woman was LuAn Halter-Mitchell, with whom they had briefly spoken a few times during the event and with whom Shirley had the honor of taking a photograph. LuAn greatly admired Juliet. Anyone could clearly tell how loving a mother Juliet was by the way Shirley acted and looked.

"It's too dark, loud, and crowded in there," Juliet said distastefully once they arrived at the nightclub's entrance. "Let's leave. I'm really tired."

"Yes, let's go," agreed Shirley, who found the nightclubs unappealing. It was time to call it a day. They had had enough adventures for one day, and plus, they would have to get up early to catch their plane tomorrow morning.

Was it all for real? With thousands of sounds and memories swimming through her head, it was hard for Shirley to know.

# Chapter XVII
# Never an Ending, Always a Beginning

Shirley sleepily fluttered her eyes open. Something had snatched her away from her dreamworld. Then her eyes shot wide open. "Mom! What time is it?" She heard Juliet scurrying hither and thither in the room.

"It's 9:30," Juliet answered under a gasp of air. "We'll be late."

"Oh, gosh!" Shirley was now wide awake and alert. They had only half an hour left to get downstairs. Juliet had scheduled transportation to pick them up at ten to get to the airport for their flight at 12:50. "You should have woken me up!" She knew Juliet always let her sleep till the last minute, for she did not have the heart to wake her; then, she would work extra fast, but still gently, to get her ready. "When did you get up?"

"Not too long ago, actually. I didn't fall asleep till quite late." Juliet sounded tired.

At precisely ten, Juliet pushed Shirley out the hotel. Neither of them ate a single bite; they simply threw some clothes on. Fortunately, Shirley did not have to use the toilet, not surprisingly since she had barely eaten for two straight days.

"Where is the transportation? It's ten already." Juliet muttered. She asked a bell man, and he told her that it would be there. It was actually 9:50 — Juliet's watch was ten minutes fast.

Fifteen minutes later, a wheelchair-accessible vehicle parked in front of them. The driver secured Shirley at the back, so she did not have to be carried onto the seat.

"Our trip is almost over," said Shirley, both relieved and wistful. She thoroughly enjoyed the experience, but it would be nice to be back home, where she could use her commode whenever she wished. They had a wall lift in the bedroom, as well as one in the bathroom.

By eleven, mother and daughter, with their hands clasped together, waited for the airport loudspeaker to announce their flight. A few planes, Shirley heard, were delayed, for New York was experiencing bad weather. She hoped that their own flight would not be delayed. She hoped in vain, for the loudspeaker informed their fellow passengers that there would be an hour of delay. Shirley could not help but sigh. Then her sigh turned to one of contentment.

What an experience it had been! She could and would never ever forget about it, not a single detail. But their adventure was not yet over; they still had to fly home.

Shirley thought about their one-hour delay, and felt grateful. What was it compared to hours, or even days, of delay, like what many travelers had experienced? No, she could not complain.

Forty minutes later, however, they were allowed to board the plane. Juliet and a male flight attendant performed a two-man lift on Shirley.

"Ah!" Shirley screamed. Pain shot from her legs. Juliet had almost lost her grip on Shirley's legs, causing the agonizing pain. Juliet's hands had lost energy after she carried Shirley those two times yesterday. She had felt a tendon in her hand snapping.

"Is she okay?" the concerned flight attendant asked. Shirley was crying in pain.

"Yes, she is. Thank you very much."

"I'm sorry about that."

Juliet shook her head. He had lifted Shirley well; it was she who had hurt her. She turned to the sniffling Shirley, who was drying her eyes and blowing her nose. "Are you okay?"

Shirley weakly nodded. Her allergies had not bothered her since they went away. She had taken an anti-histamine when they arrived at the hotel two days ago. Was it really two days ago? It felt as though at least a week had gone by.

The plane began to turn around and drive down the runway roughly thirty minutes later. Shirley heard the flight attendant saying that there were fifty planes before theirs heading to New York. She always listened with full concentration to every word the plane loudspeaker said every time they traveled on planes.

Shirley felt her spine tingling when her favorite part of the ride began: the takeoff. She wished that she could see outside, as she had always enjoyed when they went to China. "A guy is recording the scene at his window," Juliet told her.

The engine crescendoed before the plane zoomed down the runway. "What's the speed?" Shirley asked Juliet. Each passenger had a screen in front of them that showed a map of where their plane was, their traveling speed and altitude.

"129."

Shirley soon felt the plane tilting. She saw the

takeoff in her mind's eye. Like a bird, its legs tucked into its body as it became airborne.

"What's the speed now?"

"297."

Shortly, Shirley felt that her seat was leveled again. During the flight, Shirley kept track of the speed and altitude. They mostly flew above 35,000 feet above ground, and their fastest speed was around 585.

Their scheduled landing was supposed to be 9:05 p.m. Eastern Time, and surprisingly, the one-hour delay in takeoff had delayed the arrival time only by half an hour. Juliet had made a call to their taxi driver, informing him of the delay.

They lifted Shirley onto the wheelchair with no trouble this time, and they had an assistant to help them out off the airport. Juliet made another call to the taxi driver, who said that he was there waiting for them. But when they got outside, Juliet did not see the van anywhere, so she called again. "Where are you?"

"I'm right here," he answered.

"Where? I don't see you." Juliet searched far and wide but could not locate his vehicle.

"I am right here," he said again, just in front of her very eyes.

Juliet burst out laughing. "You're right *here*!"

He laughed, too. Shirley followed suit.

He carried Shirley onto the back seat, put everything in the back, and off they were, to their home sweet home.

In less than two hours, their adventure would officially be over. A chapter would end, and a new chapter would soon follow: BookExpo America 2007.

\*\*\*

"Wow!" exclaimed Shirley breathlessly. Mother and daughter were lying in bed, using their last ounce of energy to ruminate about the past three days. It was two in the morning, two hours after they returned home from their trip. "We have made it."

"We didn't do bad, eh?"

"Not at all." Shirley giggled, but her giggles quickly turned into a groan when she moved her legs. Her knees had been sacrificed in the trip greatly. She had held the heavy carry-on too long, and it had crushed her knees. She had not expected that to happen; it had felt perfectly fine at first since most of the weight was put on her lap. But her joints were much too delicate for even a bit of pressure for a short period of time. The slanted plane seats had not helped her knees, either. The position had badly hurt her knees throughout the flights. Juliet had rubbed Chinese medicinal ointment on her knees. It had cured Juliet's foot pain, so she hoped that it could treat Shirley's knee pain.

A smile was on Shirley's lips right before tiredness overcame her being. And before Juliet entered her own world of dreams and fancies, she thought of their next event.

# Spirituality: the Secret to Everlasting Success

## How One Blind and Physically Disabled Individual Views Spirituality and Its Effects on Success

How did you start your success quest and where are you now?

I believe I started my success quest when I was a baby. True, I was too young to knowingly pursue success, but I did have to become successful in overcoming my disability. So my first experience of success was enduring tremendous physical pain. I was nicknamed the Happy Baby when I was thirteen months old, despite the agonizing pain. My road to success has led me to where I am now, a successful writer, motivational speaker, poet, and advocate, to empower others to be successful as well.

Have you ever come to the brink of giving up, when things seem too overwhelming to handle?

No, not in the least, ever. I am too much madly in love with life to give it up. Life is my best friend, a family member. We all have silly arguments with our family and friends, but do we give up on them afterward? No. So it should be the same with life. Life is a gift God gives me, the most precious gift ever. When you are given a special gift, would you not want to do your best to care for it? Life is simply too precious, too beautiful to be wasted. When you're given life, you should cherish it. I cherish my life, I hold on to every minute and don't let the happy moments pass me by.

What does it mean to be spiritual? And why is spirituality so important?

In life, everything is divided into mainly two categories: the spiritual and the worldly. What belong to the spiritual realm are everlasting. They do not know time; they do not know age. They withstand all trials and tribulations. Those who welcome spiritual elements--long-suffering love, unconditional gratitude, undemanding hope, unwavering faith, and invaluable values--will achieve true success and happiness that will last well beyond the life in this world, while leaving a legacy.

The worldly, on the other hand, give you only earthly success: wealth, power, and fame. When you die, they die with you. What good is a roomful of money when you are dead? When we live, we need to collect treasures that will last forever so we can enjoy happiness forever. Many times, we are so focused on achieving what our flesh wants, forgetting that whatever our flesh achieves will die with our flesh.

So being a spiritual person, embracing the spiritual aspects, will lead you to an enduring, fulfilling life. We are here to strengthen our spirits, to establish and hold on tightly to our faith in Jesus Christ, and to learn what Heavenly Father wants from us, so we can return His love and live by His almighty rule, eternally.

How does being spiritual help you conquer negativity or challenges in life?

Overcoming negativity is not necessarily about making a physical difference. Many times, we cannot physically change the situation we are in. I lost my eyesight, and I cannot magically make myself see again. Conquering negativity is about making a psychological difference for your spirit. By being happy when I am blind, I am successfully conquering negativity.

A method of spiritually conquering negativity is finding the positive side to a negative situation. I know it can be quite difficult to always be able to find the good side of something bad; you will have to look at your situation from every angle. While at times, the good thing does not come out of the bad until some time has passed. After I lost my eyesight, I became an author and motivational speaker; that was the good that came from the bad. This way, I am able to touch others in ways I could not have if I had not lost my eyesight; at least, it would not have been so soon or exactly in this way. Another example is that I have periods of severe insomnia, and it is during my insomnia that many of my great writing ideas come to me, so that is the positive side of insomnia. In life, there are always something good and something bad happening at the same time, and there is always a positive side to the negative, and even a negative side to the positive. And there are times where the bad actually become the good and vice versa. So in actuality, it can be too hard at times for us to judge what is truly good or bad. What we can do is always try to look on the bright side and do our best to live our best, and put all faith in God—that is the secret that gets me going; everything else is just strategy!

So it is all about the attitude?

They say attitude is everything; but I say your desires are everything. You need desires to help you conquer negativity. You may say, of course, that's easy. But surprisingly, their desires are the first barrier many people cannot achieve. Let me say that if you are not really overcoming negativity as best as you could have, that tells me that your desires are not strong enough, no matter what you say. You need one hundred percent desires; even ninety-nine percent desires will eventually make you fail. We all get into silly, inconsequential arguments sometimes. We could have ended those fights as quickly as they got started, but we didn't because our desire to end them was not strong enough. Each party wanted to win the fights, to be the one to get the last word in; their desire to win overpowered their desire to end the arguments. So the key is to use the right kind of desires; we all have desires, but we need to use the good ones and let them rule over all other desires.

What does it mean to be truly successful? And can you share with us some of your tips to success?

To me, success does not mean wealth and fame; success is all about being a successful human being. In order to be truly successful in life, you need to first establish your values.

What qualities do you hold highest? What traits do you want to have and be associated with? Think of what qualities are important to you and hold firm to them. Your values are what you will base your life's decisions on. You will make goals around your core values. For example, my value is goodness, so I make goals that will accomplish my value. I will be satisfied with having achieved that value if nothing else.

Two plus two equals four. If you believe that two plus two equals everything and anything, then you are bound to encounter problems in your life. Your values create a lasting, enduring spiritual environment. Nothing you gain in life is ever guaranteed; everything you own—your car, your house, and even your friends and family—can be taken away from you. But nothing can take away your values if you do not let them. No one can destroy your values unless you destroy them yourself. Your values are what will guide you in the right paths in life.

Besides establishing your firm values, my golden rule to be truly successful is: Do your best in everything you do. Many people do a mediocre job and expect to be successful; they depend on luck to get them successful. But in the long term, luck will not bring you far. In life, no matter what position you are in—as a parent, a child, a teacher, a doctor—do your best in being your best. And make the most of what you have. If you only have a spoon and a fork, use the fork to comb your hair and use the spoon to play music. Hey, some people do not even have a spoon and a fork. In my case, I lost my eyesight, but I still have my fingers so I can type; I still can hear, I am still alive. I use all those wonderful factors to become an award-winning author, motivational speaker, published poet, advocate, and I continue to love the life I live.

How do you live without limitations?

Let us face it, everyone has limitations. But the thing is that we can live in a way that does not let our limitations have the most negative effect on our lives. We need to live in a way that is most beneficial, with the least hindrance, and that is by limiting your limitations.

For example, if you are good in math but not good as a cook, focus on your talent in math, instead of focusing on your inability to cook. So focus on your strong points, not on your weak points. Concentrate on what you are able to do, not what you are unable to do. If you lose your left hand, you will not try to continue using this phantom hand to do everything. You will instead use your right hand and train it to do the things your left hand was able to do. I am blind; that is a fact. That is a limitation I have, and I will not deny it. But what I do is to limit my limitation, disable my disability, by focusing my attention on what things I am still able to do and enjoy doing without my eyesight. When you are good at something, then do it and do your very best with it.

# Chapter XVIII
# More Adventures in the Big Apple

"Are you sure that's him?" Shirley, dressed in a black and white summer dress, fingered the envelope in her hand, as the other held tightly to the photograph in a frame.

"Yes, I recognize him," replied Juliet, pushing Shirley toward the table where Robert F. Kennedy Jr sat. It was Friday, June 1, the first day of BookExpo America 2007, and Robert was signing his new children's book, *American Hero: The Story of Joshua Chamberlain and the American Civil War*, at the autographing area. The event was held in New York at the Jacob K. Javits Conventional Center again, so Juliet and Shirley were able to attend it.

"Hi, Shirley!" Robert promptly greeted, reading the badge that was pinned to Shirley's dress, which displayed her publishing company, Dance with Your Heart! Publishing, under which she had published *Waking Spirit*.

"Hi, Mr. Kennedy, it's a great honor to meet you!"

Juliet was next to greet him. She took the photograph from Shirley and showed it to Robert, who exclaimed, "Oh, that's Teddy!" The photograph was of Senator Edward Kennedy; Dr. Ling, Shirley's late step-grandfather, who was a psychiatrist and neurologist; and Kwi Show, taken around 1982. "Would you like me to sign it?"

"Yes, please," said Juliet, smiling.

Robert added his autograph to the photograph on the light-colored dress Kwi Show wore—the only light place on the picture. And it so happened to be that the photograph had no covering, so he conveniently signed on the photograph itself. If it had had a covering, he would not have been able to sign it.

Shirley held out the envelope. "Here's a letter to Senator Kennedy; I'd greatly appreciate it if you could pass it to him." She wrote a letter to the senator to share with him the two issues she was advocating: parental rights in children's medical care and aide/caregiver screening and monitoring for students with special needs or the disabled people in general. But above all, she wrote it to thank the senator for helping Kwi Show immigrate to America in 1978.

They thanked him before leaving. But less than a minute later, they returned to his table. They forgot one other thing.

"Would you like to take a picture with Shirley?" asked Juliet. "You can stay there. I can push Shirley over." Each autographing table was about four feet tall, and they had a raised area for seating. But Robert got down from his seat and kneeled next to Shirley for the shot.

They thanked him again and left. "He has a very kind countenance," Juliet told Shirley when they were out of earshot.

"I'm so glad I have a photo with him."

Unlike the last BookExpo America they went to, Shirley did not plan to ask anyone to buy the rights to her books. She realized that it did not work this way. Besides, she quite enjoyed being her own publisher. However, that did not mean that she was not there for publicity: the first thing she did when she arrived at the center was bring a pile of the media releases announcing *Waking Spirit*'s Indie Excellence award to the press room. She also had the book exhibited and represented by the Combined Book Exhibit in the New Title Showcase, International Publishers Alliance, ForeWord Magazine, and Publishers Marketing Association, of which she was a member. At this attendance, She planned to spend the time to meet some of the publishing professionals she met online, a few of the celebrities that were scheduled to appear at their publishing booths, and mainly for her own book signing on Saturday at the autographing area, followed by an Author's Studio interview. She was to sign *Waking Spirit* at table thirty-four, the last table in line where it was most spacious, precisely at two in the afternoon for a full hour.

"So what's next?" Juliet asked.

"Check the schedule I gave you." Shirley had made a schedule for all three days of what they would do and whom they would meet. "We'll have plenty of time before my meeting at 2:30." She was to meet a woman from *The Book Standard* in front of the International Rights Center. She would interview Shirley on what she had been up to in the book business.

From the schedule, Juliet saw that Shirley would meet the *Chicken Soup for the Soul* team at their booth at four, followed by attending a keynote event in the Special Events Hall at 5:15, when Alan Greenspan, the former chairman of Federal Reserve, would be interviewed by his wife. "We have nothing to do now. Do you want something to eat?"

As usual, Shirley said, "No." Even though she usually had a poor appetite, it had recently been nearly non-existent because of her menstruation; she was on the last day of her period.

"But let's go to the food court to rest. I may like to bring something back to the hotel."

At the food court, Juliet videotaped Shirley, who briefly introduced herself and explained where she was. At two, they started off toward the International Rights Center. Upon arrival, Juliet snapped a few photographs of Shirley and videotaped her and the place. As she was recording, the woman from *The Book Standard* came up to Shirley. After an introduction, they went to a quieter place to talk.

"In America, parents risk losing custody of their children forever when they disagree with doctors' recommended treatments, or even when they want a second opinion," Shirley told her during the fast-paced interview. "This nightmare has happened to many parents, including to my mother twice. She lost custody of me only after disagreeing with doctors' recommended treatments, and those treatments would have sent me to my grave. The last case in 1990 made international headlines, and she was on CBS *This Morning* with Paula Zahn. When doctors ask yes or no, parents should have the right to say no. I want to help today's loving parents protect the children of our future, and to put an end to this injustice."

Shirley showed a copy of her forthcoming parental rights advocacy book, which still needed to be edited. The woman jotted everything down, and soon, the interview ended. Both parties thanked the other as each went their separate way.

***

"I suppose this is the green room," said Juliet, pushing Shirley inside. "It's not at all green." It was the following day, and Shirley promptly arrived in the green room before her signing was to start. It was only one, so she and Juliet quietly chatted. Then a gentleman walked up to Shirley.

"Hi, Shirley, I'm Dave Holton."

Shirley took out her hand. "It's so nice to meet you, Mr. Holton. Thank you so much for everything!" She gave him an appreciative smile. Dave, who was the coordinator for the autographing program, had gone out of his way to personally take care of the three boxes of her books, receiving them at his own place and bringing them to the autographing site, without having Juliet experience any trouble. Without his kind offer, Juliet would have mailed the large boxes of books on her own. Shirley thought that was extraordinarily kind of him, and she would always be grateful to him.

Another gentleman came up to Shirley and told her that they had a low table just right for her height and wanted to know if she would like that, to which Shirley said, "That will be great! Thank you."

When two o'clock arrived, Juliet got Shirley situated at her table, and got out two custom-made rubber stamps, one of her autograph, and the other of the short message unique to *Waking Spirit*: Dance to the music of life!

"Oh, here come some people," Juliet announced.

Shirley greeted the first person and asked, "To whom would you like me to sign it?" She repeated the question to each person.

After they left, a few more people followed a moment later. By the end of the hour, Shirley had signed over thirty books. She was pleased to have signed this many as she was relatively unknown. "Many authors here did not have that many visitors," Juliet told her.

"Next is my Author's Studio interview," Shirley told Juliet after they left the autographing area. They would return to the area at the end of the day, so someone could bring the leftover books to their van. "At 4:10, so we still have time left." They rested until 3:40 and headed off toward the recording studio. Shirley was delighted to learn that they could interview her earlier, so in a matter of minutes, the interview was over.

"I wish you the best with everything," the interviewer told Shirley before they left.

The last thing on Shirley's agenda for the day was a meeting with Tina Louise, who had played Ginger Grant on *Gilligan's Island*, a sitcom Shirley watched when she was little. Tina was to appear at her publisher's booth for her new children's book, *When I Grow Up*, at four, so they went straight to her booth from the studio.

"I think she's about to leave. I'm going to fetch her now," Juliet said, before walking over to Tina, who had a bag over her slender shoulder. "My daughter would like to meet you," she said.

Tina knelt down in front of Shirley, who held out her hand. "It's great to meet you. I really enjoyed your show and I loved your character!"

"Thank you," came the quiet reply.

"I'd really like to take a photo with you. Could

we?"

"Oh, yes, of course." Tina turned to face the camera Juliet held in front of her.

Soon afterward, Juliet and Shirley returned to the autographing area to meet whoever would bring the books to their van. Shirley was pleased how the day ended. Mother and daughter happily left the center, ready for the final day at BookExpo America 2007.

On the last day, they stayed at the center only three hours and left by noon. They had missed eating breakfast during the authors breakfast, where Rosie O'Donnell was the master of ceremony. Shirley had hoped that she could speak with her personally, but Rosie left soon after she spoke to the audience. For the first time, both Shirley and Juliet wanted breakfast, so they had it at the food court outside the Special Events Hall where the authors breakfast was held.

After returning to their hotel, Shirley needed to use the commode for the first time since they had been in the city. Juliet managed to carry her onto the commode, which they had brought with them. The bed was higher than the commode, so she used a sliding motion to get her on.

This time, they spent a night before leaving for home, for the bed was not hard, yet it was still not comfortable for Shirley's arthritic waist.

# Chapter XIX
# Appreciating the Purity of Life

A week following BookExpo America 2007, Juliet and Shirley were once again away from home, but not too far away. It was June 15, and Shirley wore a wide grin as she greeted people during her third book signing at Borders Books, Music & Cafe; the signing had been scheduled in January for March 16, but it had been postponed because of a snowstorm. The people she welcomed to her table were mostly friends, including one of their next-door neighbors, who brought along Florence, a co-worker of his. There was not a minute of silence among the small group of friends before it was time for everyone to leave. For the first time, Shirley did not give any talks. She had wanted her audience to be composed of mostly strangers. She did not feel that it was necessary to talk to those who already knew her. Plus, having to talk loudly in a wide open space tired her a great deal, so she did not choose to talk unless it was necessary. Even though she did not make any profit this time, she felt that it was worthwhile. At least, she had one more event to add to her memory book deep in her heart. Not all events or activities had to be monetarily successful in order to be successful. This occasion, like any other she and Juliet ever had, was successful for many reasons: they had fun, they had done their utmost, and they had built on their memories. That is what the purity of life is all about.

***

"Folks, I want to get right into this tonight because I have a fantastic person, her name is Shirley Cheng. Shirley, welcome."

Shirley, her ears ringing somewhat from the excitement, answered Phil Harris. "Hi Phil, good evening, thank you so much for having me." It was three days after her book signing. She had scheduled this radio interview on *All Things That Matter* with the host in April. She felt that it was just yesterday; time certainly flew.

"My pleasure. I'm just going to give everybody a quick rundown about you, Shirley, and then we are going to jump right into this. Shirley Cheng, award winning writer, finalist in the New Age Non-Fiction of the national Indie Excellence 2007 Book Awards, miracle survivor, inspiring author, and contributing author of thirteen books by the age of twenty-three, poet, motivational speaker, self-empowerment expert, and co-author in the best selling *Wake Up, Live the Life You Love* book series, and board member of World Positive Thinkers Club. Her Web site by the way is www.shirleycheng.com. Here's a quote from Shirley, 'Although I'm blind, I can see far and wide, even though I'm disabled, I can climb high mountains, let the ropes of hope haul you high!' Shirley, you have an absolutely fantastic background and we could probably spend the whole show talking about some of your accomplishments, but for the sake of our listeners, while we may get into that a little bit more, what I really want you to focus on is, how do you do it?"

"How do I do it? Well, that's what everyone asks, well, most of them anyway. What I tell them is that life inspires me. Actually, I love life, I'm crazy about life, I feel that life is simply too precious to be wasted. When you are given life, you should cherish it; I know I cherish my life. I value it every minute. I hold onto the happy moments and don't let them pass me by, I don't dwell on the negativity that surrounds me, I choose to move forward by focusing on the good things I do have at the present and the positive side of things, so life lets me move on and move forward. I enjoy every minute of my existence. I thank God for everyday, I thank God for the countless blessings I have."

"Basically, you talk about a positive mental attitude, you've managed to get through—I'm not even going to call them disabilities because I don't think they are, I think they were gifts to you, Shirley. You were born with—you may have some things that other people label as disabilities but it seems to me that those have been gifts to you to help you soar and to let your spirit rise above anything that comes your way."

"Absolutely, my personal motto is 'I'm not disabled, I'm ultra-abled.'"

Phil laughed. "You talk about negative versus positive thinking and most people probably have no clue about some of the things you have probably have had to experience when you were growing up. So many people tend to go through life with very negative attitudes; I mean everything gets them down. The coffee's too cold in the morning, somebody cuts them off on their way driving to work, the boss might be snapping at them, the weather isn't right and the world is going to hell in a hand basket. How do you get people to get over that mental mindset?"

Shirley knew what he was going to ask even before he asked it; most hosts had had the same questions, and she had been so used to answering them that she could answer them when she was half-awake. "There are always two roads to choose from in life, the road to happiness, which leads to ability, success, and self-fulfillment; and the road to unhappiness, the road to misery, which leads you to disability. You have the power to disable yourself or enable yourself. If you choose the road to misery, you will put yourself in a much more miserable situation then the one you are already in, and also being miserable, you are going to make others around you more miserable. Also, happiness attracts happiness, the same goes with misery. Misery attracts misery, so when I choose my road, I ask myself 'Hey, do I want to be happy or do I want to be unhappy, which will make my situation worse.' So I choose to be happy because of the good things I do have, I try to think of how I can make the situation better, and whenever a door is closed to me, I find another door to open."

"You make it sound so simple, I'm sure people listening have got to be sitting there saying, 'Wait a minute, like I said, when I have an argument with my wife or the dog pees on the floor, how do you expect me to have such a positive attitude?' How do I get over the negative forces that sometimes impinge upon us from the moment we open our eyes?"

"Think about it, it could be worse than it is already. You could be homeless, you could not have that dog, and you could be 'pet-less.' So instead of complaining that the dog peed on your floor, you say 'Oh, I have a pet that loves me unconditionally, so hey, it's okay if he peed.'" Shirley's neck was starting to get stiff. Because of her arthritis, she used the telephone by balancing the receiver on her right shoulder, as she held it with her left hand. And she could use only one of the several telephones they had, for it had the lightest receiver, and its design fit most comfortably on her shoulder. She could not hold most of the telephones this way to reach her ear. As with much of the technology, gadgets were getting smaller and smaller, and the small-sized receivers made it hard for her to hold it, let alone use it for an interview.

"What about the person who is homeless, though? How does the person—you obviously started with what some people would say a lot of strikes against you, but you're saying, 'No, uh-uh that's not for me, these are strikes for me.' From the person who is homeless, the person that may not be experiencing the highest level of employment or maybe they're either unemployed and facing harsh economic issues, and they're like, 'How do those people who are inundated every moment with negative thoughts and ideas about themselves and about the world, how do they dig themselves out of that mental hole?'"

"They have to—you have to have the determination first of all to get out of that rut. If you don't, then you are always going to be stuck in that hole. So focus on what you need to do to get out of that hole. If you don't think about how you can do it, you might never do it. You may never accomplish anything. You have to plan and act upon your plan."

"Yeah, that's true, if you begin to say, 'Gee, I have a terrible situation,' it's kind of an oh-poor-me attitude which tends to just generate oh poor me."

"Yes, it doesn't do anything for you; it doesn't

get you out of the bad situation."

Phil asked one question after another. There was never a pause during the interview. Shirley knew that hosts must need to possess not only a quick mind but a quizzical mind as well. Later in the interview, Phil asked, "Well, okay. So, I have to ask this because anytime I send you an E-mail I get an E-mail right back, and I absolutely adore you for that. Do you have a special typewriter, how do you know what I'm saying?"

"I use a screen reader. It's computer software that reads what's on the screen and tells you which keys you type. So, it reads E-mails to me and I type. I can type with only my two index fingers because of my severe arthritis, but I manage quite well at about sixty words per minute."

"How many?"

"Sixty words per minute."

Phil laughed. "I'm lucky if I do twenty and that's with ten fingers. That's incredible, two fingers and you do sixty words per minute and blind to boot. Okay, obviously, there is somebody not dealing with his or her limitations by any stretch of the imagination."

"Where do you feel the inspiration comes from?" Phil asked, referring to her books.

It was a usual question, so Shirley gave him her usual answer. "Life."

Phil then commented that a lot of people are afraid to be responsible for their lives. "What's your experience with that?"

"I'm not afraid at all of any sort of responsibility. I love to be a leader, not a follower, and I just feel that life gives me this privilege to live so I want to do my best to show God that I am honored to be alive. I am honored to take this position, to have the responsibility to care for my own life and hopefully to help others on the road."

Phil asked about improving one's health naturally, and Shirley replied by saying, "I believe being happy makes you not only spiritually better, but physically better as well. Happiness motivates you, misery does not, misery glues you to the same spot. Laugh more, smile more. I tell people to smile, it's the sweetest treat you can treat yourself, and the best part is that there are no calories."

"You're right; there are no calories for smiling." Phil laughed.

Five minutes later, the thirty-minute interview ended with Phil saying, "Folks, we're talking to Shirley Cheng, an absolute inspiration to anybody and everybody out there in the world. Her Web site is www.shirleycheng.com. Visit her site, pick up her books. An absolute brilliant light in what is sometimes a sea of darkness here."

When it was time for Shirley to hang up, she could not: her arm had fixed to its position. She remembered an episode on *I Love Lucy* where Lucy was using Fred as a model for her sculpture, and by the time she finished, Fred could not straighten out. He said that he might as well go to bowling in his position. Well, she might as well play the violin in her position. Her head was wide and her ears were small, so it was not a good combination for headphones. She never liked using speakerphones, so her choices had been greatly narrowed to the telephone, which she slowly untangled herself. It was her twenty-fifth radio interview; it, she decided, would be the last one for now. She wanted to take a short vacation from the interviews, which did not bring her any sales, as far as she knew. And only one interview she had increased hits to her Web site, and it was her short interview on *Daddy Dave's Hollywood Diner*, a music show on XM Satellite Radio. It had brought her twenty hits just after her Web site was announced on the show, and twenty more when the show was rebroadcast.

Her thoughts were turned to an upcoming event once she was free from the telephone. She was to hold a book signing during the New York Book Festival in Central Park over the weekend. She and Juliet would set out to the city on Friday, June 22, and would go to the park the following morning. It was a whole day's event, so she hoped that her mother would have the strength to stay out that long. The event would prove to be challenging for several reasons — they would have to get her books to their tent, find a parking space for their van, and no one knew how far they would have to walk. But fortunately, they had the manual wheelchair, so Juliet would not have to struggle with a heavy wheelchair on the congested streets.

Shirley had entered *Waking Spirit* in the book contest sponsored by the festival, and to her immeasurable delight, she received Honorable Mention in the Poetry category. She had received the good news just two days after her Borders book signing. She had wanted to attend their awards ceremony held at the Speakeasy restaurant, but she sadly found out that the party would be in the basement. There was no way she could attend it unless they could lift her down...

# Chapter XX
# NYC, Home of Adventures

"Pearl, the stairs seem very sturdy," Juliet assured Shirley as two men was about to lift her down to the restaurant basement. They had agreed to have two strong gentlemen lift Shirley, so she could attend the awards ceremony with her fellow award winners to celebrate their victory. Shirley was using the wheelchair her late step-grandfather had used, for it was in one single piece, making it an ideal wheelchair to be lifted; the arms, unlike the ones on Shirley's new manual wheelchair, could not be removed. Shirley held onto the arms as they lifted her down. She lifted her feet and kept them as close to the wheelchair as possible to prevent the man in front of her from bumping into them.

"Thank you so much!" Juliet and Shirley said when they arrived down in the basement. They were both extremely grateful to them. They had made it possible for Shirley to attend the ceremony.

Juliet took out her camera and said, "Let's take some photos since it hasn't started," to which Shirley nodded. She snapped several shots until the room became noisy. They had been the first to arrive, but now about a dozen of people filled the room.

About an hour later, the event's coordinator stepped in front of the room to start the ceremony. He announced the list of winners and Honorable

Mentions, and if any of them was present, asked them to go up to say a few words.

Shirley waited in anticipation for her turn to share her happiness with the others. Her heart pounded when her turn arrived. The man held the microphone to her as she said, "Good evening, everyone. I bet everyone's doing fabulous, right?"

They all shouted, "Yes!"

"When I received the E-mail telling me that I received Honorable Mention, well, let's just say that I was floating on Cloud Nine." Shirley detected flashes in front of her. Someone videotaped her short speech.

"Aww," came from the audience.

"So what inspires me? Life inspires me...life is simply too precious to be wasted..." Shirley then finished with, "Dance with your heart to the music of life!"

Everyone broke out in loud applause. After the announcements were made, several people came up to Shirley and congratulated her. The grand-prize winner, a Hollywood actress and screenwriter, told her, "Your speech gave me goosebumps!"

Soon afterward, the ceremony ended, and two different gentlemen lifted Shirley back up to the main floor, which boomed with music. It was an evening never to be forgotten, that was for certain. Shirley happily fell asleep that night, awaiting the next promising day.

***

"The van is just entering the park—we came at the right time!" Juliet was directed to follow the van, which would lead them to the portion of the park where their booth was located. It was almost nine in the morning; if they had come even one minute later, they would have missed the van and not known where to go. Two boxes of Shirley's books sat behind at the back of Juliet's van. Shirley had contacted them before the event, and they had told her that their staff members could help vendors unload.

When they arrived, Juliet was glad to know that their booth, along with many other booths, were under the same large tent on solid ground, not grass, so she would not experience a hard time pushing Shirley. They helped Juliet unload the books, and Juliet set up their table. But before they could situate themselves, Juliet had to park their van somewhere else. They had started out luckily, so hopefully luck would continue to be on their side as they searched for a parking garage.

When they drove out of the park, Juliet immediately spotted a parking garage by the entrance. "It's down a hill. How am I going to push you up if I park there?" As Juliet was mulling over the situation, she saw a man by the garage and asked if he could help. To her delight, he told her to drop Shirley off there and he could drive her van down. He handed her his card, so she could call him when they needed the van again. Luck was definitely on their side.

Juliet pushed Shirley back to their tent; the walk took around seven minutes. Juliet got Shirley's poster, the same one they had been using since early 2006, upright on its stand, and put a few copies of each of her books in front of Shirley on the table. Next, she took out the rubber stamps and the fliers Shirley had printed out about her Indie Excellence finalist status. From the small bag tied to her wheelchair, Shirley took out a deck of business cards. She held a pen in her hand. She was more than ready for the seven-hour festival to begin around ten.

As hours passed, to everyone's disappointment, they seldom made a sale. The table next to Shirley's had sold only one copy thus far, whereas she had sold none. Hundreds of visitors had passed through their tent, only glancing at each table before leaving. "What's really selling here is the food," noted Juliet. "Food is always the best sell anywhere."

Around three, both Juliet and Shirley were getting tired and bored. They had not made a single sale, and found out that many others had had the same fate, except for a table to their left which had sold two books.

"Mom, I think I have my period," Shirley said in almost a whisper, even though no one around them understood Mandarin.

"You do?"

"I think so, but it's a few days early."

"Then I have to put tissues under you."

"But how? We can't do it here!"

"No one is looking."

"But they'll start looking when you're stuffing tissues in my pants!" They were surrounded by people, with booths to their left and right and behind them, and visitors walking past them all the time.

"Well, don't worry about it then. I'll just wash your underwear and pants when we get back to the hotel, and change you into the spare underwear and pants I brought."

"I'll see if I can hold it in. It's very light."

"Don't worry about it," repeated Juliet.

After a while had passed, they decided to leave; they were not making any progress, and Shirley did not want to get too much reddie on her underwear, which would make it hard for Juliet to wash, so Juliet packed everything up, and together, they left their tent. They asked if someone could help them, but they were told that no one was allowed to leave until five, when they would help people to load their books to their vehicles, so the pair headed back to their booth.

Back at their table, Juliet set everything up again and waited for five o'clock to arrive. Just then, a woman was going around the tables, interviewing individual authors. Juliet told the woman that she could interview Shirley. "Good thing we didn't leave," Juliet said to Shirley, who nodded.

When the woman got to Shirley's table, she introduced herself as having a new Web site where they showcased video clips of authors, and asked if Shirley would like to be interviewed and have the taped interview on the Web site for all to see.

"I'd love to!" answered Shirley.

The video-taped interview lasted about ten minutes wherein Shirley talked about her life and her books. "You are very articulate!" exclaimed the woman. "It's the best interview I've had today! Thank you so much for agreeing to the interview. Your story is absolutely amazing."

"Thank you. I thoroughly enjoyed it."

Juliet packed up everything just before five. A worker carried the boxes away to bring to their own event's van and told them to wait by the entrance where their van would meet them to give them back their books. "So we're all set," Juliet said half to herself. She pushed Shirley back to the parking garage and made a call to the man. He promptly brought out their van and Juliet got Shirley secured in. "Good thing the

EZ-lock is working properly now!" Juliet was referring to the locking system for the wheelchair. She had had a new one installed in the van for the new manual wheelchair, and it always got stuck. At BookExpo America 2007, it had gotten stuck every time they went out, and Juliet had had ask passersby to help pull Shirley's wheelchair free from the system. The men had used great energy to pull her out. Thus, Juliet went to another dealer to get it fixed; he saw what was wrong immediately and was able to fix it on the spot.

Juliet drove to where they were told to wait. They waited for over half an hour when the van appeared. After receiving the two boxes, Juliet headed back to their hotel.

"What a long day!" Shirley yawned. She just wanted to hit the pillows when they got there. And no, she was not hungry; She had had some munchies and a fresh-fruit shake during the festival. She felt that New York City was a second home. She really had had enough traveling for now and planned that this would be her last engagement for the time being. Little did she know that they would be back in the noisy city in less than a month.

# Chapter XXI
# Pushing Onward Still

"Hmm." Shirley reread the E-mail that just arrived in her inbox.

> I am a producer working with Gary Null, the well-known health/fitness expert, lifestyle coach, NY Times Best-seller author.
> He's working on a new series and he would like to interview you for this new project.
> Please get back to me ASAP, we would love to have you on board.
>
> Congratulations for your outstanding work and achievements,

Shirley promptly replied to the E-mail, thanking Xena, the producer, for their interest and expressing her own interest in being a part of Gary's new project. A few days passed without hearing back from the producer, so Shirley wrote again, providing her telephone number this time. She had done some research on the Internet and felt that the E-mail was genuine, but she was not entirely sure. That evening, Xena called her and left a message on her answering machine, for she was not available then. In her message, she said that she would call the following day around 1:30 or 2:00. When Shirley received the message, she wrote Xena back, telling her that she would wait for her call then.

Tied to film shooting sessions, the producer could not get a chance to call Shirley the next day. A few days later, both parties finally had a chance to connect on the telephone. Shirley found out that Gary was working on a PBS film project about perfect harmony and the law of attraction, of which Phil Harris had called her incarnate, both of which Shirley could talk about because of her personal experiences, and she told Xena that she would be able to cover this in the interview.

"Is your studio wheelchair accessible?" asked Shirley. "I suppose it is."

"Yes, oh." Xena hesitated. "Actually, the filming studio is upstairs and there's no elevator."

"Hmm, then it's not accessible." Shirley was quite disappointed.

"You may laugh at this—but I think the practical way is to carry you up."

"Carry me up??" Shirley knew that depended on the staircase. "What's the staircase like? Is it steep?"

"I'm not sure. We'll work something out. I'll ask Gary about it."

Before they hung up, Xena told her that she would E-mail her the topics that Gary would cover to make sure Shirley could talk about them. Shirley repeated the conversation to Juliet, who told her that she would call the man, whom she had asked to go to Las Vegas, to help lift Shirley upstairs to the filming studio. "He ought to know another strong guy. I'll call him right now." After getting off the phone, she turned to Shirley. "Yes, he said that he could definitely find someone, and both of them could lift you. You can write the producer now to tell them that we have help."

In a few days, they scheduled Shirley to meet them in New York City at their studio on July 20, just a week away. But Juliet was starting to feel uneasy about lifting Shirley. "We don't know what the staircase is like. We don't know how steep and narrow it is and how many steps it has," muttered Juliet.

"I've asked Xena about it and she just said that she doesn't know. She guessed that the staircase has twenty-five steps and there's only one flight of stairs," said Shirley, who did not feel any more comfortable about it than Juliet.

"I really think we should do it somewhere else. Is there no other place in the city…?" Then she gasped. "Ah ha, we can do it in a hotel room where it's nice and quiet, and above all, safe!"

"That's such a great idea! Why haven't I thought of it?"

"Xena did tell you that if upstairs won't work, they could do the shooting outside, such as in a park?"

"Yes."

"Write to her now and tell her about this and that we would pay for the hotel."

Shirley did as Juliet instructed and hoped that they would embrace this idea. This way, they would be able to go alone. To their relief, Xena said that there was no problem.

On Wednesday before the shooting, Xena called Shirley for a pre-interview and it went well. She also E-mailed Shirley a new list of topics for the interview. On Thursday, Gary called for a pre-interview as well, but Shirley missed his call, so she called him back twice to no avail. "Guess we'll just go then. I can't reach him," said Shirley.

"Yes, we'll go," replied Juliet. "If they didn't

want you to go, then they should tell you right now."

***

*I hope we won't be stuck behind a car accident*, was the thought that ran through Shirley's head as they headed southward to New York City.

"I think there's a car accident ahead of us!" Juliet said a moment later.

Shirley was more than a little shocked. *I guess that's law of attraction for you*, she thought wryly. *Be careful what you think of, because you just might get it.*

To their chagrin, they were stuck in traffic for over forty minutes. But Shirley could not help but feel grateful after they passed the accident site; compared to the car pancake, as she called it, they were incalculably fortunate. The car involved in the accident was flattened to an unrecognizable extent. Shirley was scheduled to meet the production team at four o'clock at the hotel, but it was already four when they entered the city. Yet, they were not late: the production team itself had been delayed for over an hour, so they would not arrive at the hotel until thirty minutes past five.

Once inside their room, Juliet got everything ready for the shooting. "Would you be okay?"

Shirley yawned before replying. "Yes, I'll manage." She had not slept for the entire night. Why was it that whenever they needed to go out, she could not sleep? But then, she had had periods of severe insomnia that lasted weeks each time. In the current insomnia period, she had not slept well since June, and last night had been the worst. This was her first television interview, and she could hardly keep her eyes open. Her head felt heavy. In fact, every single cell in her body felt heavy. Instead of having the privilege to enjoy her first television appearance, she had to wish it away. She wished that it could be done with as soon as possible, and the shorter, the better. Her mind felt utterly empty. She had not eaten, either, for insomnia severely hindered her already poor appetite. Yet, she kept her chin high; she would do her very best.

The filming crew, which consisted of two assistants and Xena, arrived at their room before six. Gary did not come; instead, he would interview Shirley over the telephone from the speakerphone. Shirley felt more tired when she was told of this; it was the least comfortable way for her to conduct the interview, for the speakerphone would be all the way across from her, therefore, she would need to strain to hear Gary while trying to look presentable on camera. No, this was not a moment she would treasure, but certainly it would not be an unforgettable one, either.

They shone light on Shirley, but since she was extremely photophobic, they had to put umbrellas up so the light would not bother her eyes. When everything was all set, one of the assistants left and the interview began.

During the interview, Shirley felt that her mind was floating somewhere outside her body. She had to both strain to hear Gary from the speakerphone and concentrate on answering his questions. Her mouth moved mechanically to reply to each question.

She had recently written a piece titled *The Tree of Spiritual Success*, and had hoped that she could include its contents in the interview. To her delight, she found the chance to talk about her ideas on spirituality when Gary asked her what she, the person in question, should tell her child in order to teach him life lessons.

She answered the question by providing a condensed version of her piece, trying to remember the main points of her article.

" Tell your child that he needs to build a spiritual foundation in order to live a truly successful life," Shirley began, smiling into the camera. "This foundation should consist of four principles, virtues. Some people may say there are more than four. I've broken it down to four main components; other principles or elements will be derived from these four principles. This is the basic structure, in its most essential form. The shorter the formula, the easier it can be remembered, and the more often people can apply it. So it has to be sweet and simple. Ask your child to first picture a tree. I call this tree the Tree of Spiritual Success. The trunk is the foundation of four principles, and when he has the foundation planted firmly in the ground, the tree will grow. It will produce many branches, and these are the good things that come from his foundation. From these branches, even more branches will branch out and they will bear fruits. These are the fruits of his labor, the desired end results of his foundation, his achieved goals.

"The principles that make up the foundation are faith, gratitude, values, and fourth, love.

"First, tell your child to have deep faith in something, someone, or God. Tell him why it is important to have faith in God. He needs a supporter through hard times, a friend he can count on with his life, someone he can confide in without any hesitation." Shirley continued without taking pauses in between. She felt her energy leaving her body as the minutes passed.

"The second element is gratitude. Though it

may sound easy, many, many people cannot achieve total and complete gratitude. Sure, you may be grateful when the sun is shining, the skies are blue. But what if black clouds roll in and the sky decides to cry? Would you still be grateful? Would you be grateful that you had the privilege to experience the sunshine and blue sky in the past? I am referring to gratitude for every situation, for all days. You need to have gratitude during both your sunny days and your dark days. Tell your child that if he can truly be grateful while at his lowest, primitive level, while he only has himself in life, then he will be able to face any difficulties.

"The third is his values. Ask him what are his values. What things in life does he feel are important? What qualities does he want to have and be associated with? When you identify your values, qualities, you will know what truly matter to you in life. Then you can truly recognize your main goals in life. These are your fundamental goals, the goals that will affect the other goals you'll make in life. Your values are your guide, your beacon. Once you've established firm values and beliefs, you'll know exactly where you'd want to go in life. You'll have a good idea what your life's purpose is. Your values, your beliefs create reality. Focus on them. Tell your child that nothing he gains in material is guaranteed in life. People can take away his house, his car, and his money. But no one and nothing can take away his values and beliefs if he doesn't allow them to. His values and beliefs cannot be destroyed, unless he destroys them himself.

"Lastly, love. When things go wrong in people's life, or when they don't get what they want, they start complaining about life. No matter what you do, if you've made a mistake, if you've done something you regret, the sun will always shine down upon you. The sun is designed to shine on all people. Why don't you return that unconditional love?

Value life as is, in its purest form. Tell him to love the purity of life, and explain to him what the purity of life is. Well, when you think about it, most problems in life, except for natural disasters and some diseases, are caused by humans. When you brush away those man-made problems, what's left is life in its purest form." Shirley went on talking about loving oneself.

She finished by saying, "Even if others pluck fruits off your tree and eat them all up, you'll be able to bear fruits over and over again as long as your foundation is firmly planted. But even if you lose everything you've built, you'll still have the foundation from which to build again. You will also not be devastated. You've done it the first time, so you can do it again and again and again.

"Also tell him to put his best effort in everything he does in every situation. No matter what position he is in — as a parent, as a student, as a doctor, he has to do his best in being his best."

She was relieved when the interview was up, but was surprised when Gary told her to give one or two thirty-minute presentations. She agreed to doing one. She doubt that she could last longer than another half an hour.

"You did a wonderful job," the assistant told Shirley.

"I did?"

"Yes, what you said gave me shivers."

"If I had slept, I would have done five times better."

The crew was getting tired after a long day's work, so Juliet offered to order some drinks for them, as Shirley thought over what she was going to include in her thirty-minute talk. They told her that she could rest during the taping if she needed to; they would just stop the taping then resume when she was ready to continue. Thus, it was what Shirley did; she had about four brief rests. In her presentation, she shared her inspirational life story, talked about ways to live successfully without driving oneself crazy, and the effects of positive people and negative people have on others.

"Oh, I've made it!" Shirley exclaimed when they left. "Now get me onto bed!"

"You really should eat something," urged Juliet.

Shirley only had enough energy left to shake her head.

Juliet called the front desk and ask them to send someone up to help her carry Shirley onto the bed. Shirley sagged in her seat as she waited. She felt that she had had to wait fifteen minutes when the doorman at last arrived.

For the first time in weeks, Shirley fell asleep soon after she hit the pillows.

The next day, Shirley felt refreshed, more refreshed than she had been for days. Before heading straight home, Juliet drove to Gary's television studio to check out their staircase. "Oh, my goodness!" gasped Juliet. "The stairs look awful. I'm getting a closer look." She got out of the van and walked over to the building. Less than a minute later, she returned to the van. "It's such a good thing that we didn't go to their studio. The staircase looks as though it reaches to the heavens. It is very steep and very narrow. Only one person can take the stairs at a time. It would be impossible to perform a two-man lift of your wheelchair, with you on it. And it seems as though there are more than one flight of stairs."

"Wow!" came Shirley's reply. "Fortunately, you thought of the hotel idea."

"If we had come to their studio, we would have no choice but to leave. There's no way it can work out. It would be too dangerous."

On the two-hour drive home, Shirley's mind drifted into her future. She might have another speaking engagement in the near future, for Florence had called her last month with some exciting news. Florence was one who promoted any good literature she liked, so after enjoying reading *Waking Spirit*, she told the company, at which she worked, about Shirley and her motivational speaking, and they expressed an interest in having a preliminary discussion with Shirley and Juliet for possibly scheduling a speaking engagement at their center. Shirley recently answered a pre-interview questionnaire and submitted it. All she had to do now was wait for the following month to attend the preliminary discussion.

Besides that possible engagement, Shirley was more than certain that she would have many more others. What other adventures were in store for her and Juliet? To where would they travel next? Who would be the next exciting person they would meet? And would there be a world premiere for the film in which she had a part? If so, she would surely go. They had been filming quite a few celebrities and well-known figures for the project. Ah, she felt content deep inside. She liked where her career was taking her. She knew it would not fail to excite her further. She had experienced many firsts in her career, and she knew many more awaited her ahead. All she had was to simply wait patiently with an eager soul. Whatever life would bring next, she would whole-heartedly embrace it with all her might. She had loved each and every one of her adventures, even though many had brought some of the most challenging times ever for this mother-daughter team. Yet, as challenging as they were, they were the refreshing kind of challenges, not even near the horror they had gone through together years ago. These challenges were the ones they looked forward to, the ones they craved, and the ones that would bring them awards and rewards of every kind.

# A Blind and Physically Disabled Author's Secret to Happiness

Of all your achievements, what are you most proud of?

That was what a reporter wanted to know while she interviewed me for a newspaper feature. All the major accomplishments I've achieved in my twenty-five years swam through my head at lightning speed. Which is my proudest achievement?

I could tell her that I was most proud of mastering grade level after only about 180 days of school attendance. You see, owing to years of hospitalization for severe juvenile rheumatoid arthritis, I didn't receive education until age eleven, when I attended school for the first time in special education in elementary school. Back then, I only knew my ABCs and very simple English; I knew that two plus two equaled four and that three times five made fifteen. I had no idea from where rain came or why a beautiful rainbow would follow. But because of my thirst for knowledge, I devoured everything that was taught and mostly self-taught myself how to read. So after about 180 days of attendance, I mastered grade level and entered regular sixth grade in middle school.

Or I could say it is that without either eyesight

or Braille, I was able to calculate chemistry equations in my head, and complete my GED test, including mathematical calculations and problem solving, graphs, and an essay; still scoring an exceptional 3280 on the test.

Perhaps my proudest achievement is that I'm able to write, format, publish, and promote my books, and design and maintain my own Web site, as a blind award-winning author.

But all that would be a lie. None of these things is what I'm most proud of.

"That I'm happy with my life," I answered her unhesitatingly.

"There are people who seem to have everything, but they lack happiness in their lives. They envy what others have and aren't content with what they have," I explained. "But despite my disabilities and all I have to go through, I'm very happy with my life. I'm content with what I have. That's what I'm most proud of."

How does a blind and physically disabled individual find happiness?

I've learned, received, and well experienced firsthand that everything in life is divided into mainly two compartments: the worldly and the spiritual. Worldly belongings will die with your flesh, whereas the spiritual are everlasting. I also learned from the wise Teacher that the darkness, pain, and suffering of the worldly will all be things of the past, and death will be our last enemy, so it brings no fruit to those who dwell upon the passing trials and tribulations but it will be rewarding for those who use challenges as exercising machines for their minds and spirits.

Therefore, I have enthusiastically embraced the spiritual realm of life with my whole heart and soul, and it has been the foundation of my happiness despite all the high mountains I have had to scale. Specifically, the cornerstone of my bliss lies in my deep faith in Jehovah God; it has allowed me to love and appreciate the life He has graciously given me, in turn, enabling me to conquer fiery oceans and thorny jungles to come out with stars in my arms.

If your best friend gives you a special present, would you not do your very best to care for it? My life is the most precious present God has bestowed upon me, so I don't want to give it up. I cannot give it up. I must not give it up. I have the responsibility to make the most of my situation, to embrace all life has to offer, to return Heavenly Father's unconditional love by accepting a virtuous way of life, and to share the good with others. And fulfilling my responsibilities makes me the happiest gal you'll ever meet!

# Spotlight Raves
## Excerpted Reviews

*The Adventures of a Blind and Disabled Award-Winning Author* should be required reading for anyone persisting in life's challenges or desiring goals which have been elusive.

Author Shirley Cheng will definitely inspire and motivate you with her unrelenting, unstoppable drive. Never do you feel that the phrases "I can't do it" or "I don't know how to do it." are in the vocabulary of this amazing young woman. She has overcome what might be for many insurmountable odds. Severely-crippling juvenile rheumatoid arthritis at 11 months of age, being torn from her mother twice in a custody battle in the issue of parental rights to refuse undesirable medical care, and blindness at age 17 have not prevented Shirley from living a full, rich and highly-productive life. She shares with us her secrets of living optimally through her real life adventures.

Blessed with an exceptional mother, Juliet, Shirley takes us on an upfront and real journey of continual accomplishment. Her strong faith and heart of gratefulness offer a valuable lesson to be learned for all of us. "For all things I have the strength by virtue of him who imparts power to me." (Philippians 4:13.) You are holding in your hands a wonderful treasure that will surely touch your heart, kindle a roaring bonfire propelling you into your dreams.
— Susanne Morrone, Natural Health Expert, www.NaturalHealthChat.com

The world of Shirley Cheng is one of contrasts as she relishes in her varied life experiences. Her recent autobiography, *The Adventures of a Blind and Disabled Award-Winning Author*, begins with an innocent, childlike exuberance as she shares with her readers the thrill she experiences while learning to use new software programs as well as her delight even in tiresome ordeals involved in marketing her work requiring her to travel to places like BookExpo America in New York City which is an inconvenience for anyone but quite arduous for someone who is physically disabled. In spite of being confined to a wheelchair due to severe juvenile rheumatoid arthritis at only eleven months old, Shirley's zest for life is absolutely inuring. At every turn she transforms, through her vivacious joy and appreciation of life, obstacles which would thwart the average individual without any disabilities into joyous events.

Shirley makes masterful use of the design element of contrast. I would venture to guess this is due to her first love --visual art. From my point of view, as an artist who continues to enjoy the blessing of eyesight, it is very sad that Shirley lost her eyesight at the tender age of seventeen. But her positive manner of looking at every situation even embraces the loss of her eyesight as a blessing, simply because she would not have become an author if it were not for this loss. Very few of us indeed have anything like this kind of courage.

Shirley uses extreme contrast through her humble admission of the physical obstacles she must overcome on a daily basis, (let alone enduring the discomfort and inconvenience of traveling to an overnight destination) with a depth of spiritual insight reserved for the ancient bards. She explains what she must consider prior to making an overnight trip: She needs to consider whether her destination is handicapped accessible and then make arrangements with someone willing to carry her and her wheelchair up and down flights of steps; She needs to bring her own commode; She needs to consider whether she will be menstruating, or having her reddie as she refers to it; She needs to consider how and when she will be able to partake of sustenance due to a parasitic infestation she acquired when she was five months old because this infestation causes nausea; In addition to all of this she suffers from severe constipation, allergies and asthma.

Then after describing this litany of discomfitures she hits you right between the eyes with "How You Can Effectively Conquer Negativity in Five Simple Ways." In this section she makes the exquisitely selfless statement: "...I am ready to hold your hand to guide you down your rugged journey..." and then immediately injects a word that I personally love: "...'gently' showing you how to choose which roads to travel, so that you, too, can go for your own gold medals in life." This kind of humble, gentleness of spirit is indeed rare because it is guided by truth and love; authentic love that always gives and never takes. The speech she gave to the Lions Club alone is worth purchasing her autobiography. And her use of humor, even regarding her physical drawbacks, introduces a delicate air of levity to her story as later in her book she writes: "...it would be nice to be back home, where she could use her commode whenever she wished."

Shirley and I hold a common affinity. She like I have an extraordinary and loving mother. I cherish the words I read several years ago: "A mothers prayers are the most powerful prayers of all." When I was going through my darkest time, my mom went to a nearby church and sat there for hours praying for my well-being. I am convinced that if it were not for my mothers prayers, I would not be here writing this review today. Shirley's mom, Juliet Cheng courageously stood her ground and fought for the very life of her beloved daughter. As Shirley says in her book: "Maternal love is definitely the greatest love that has ever existed." I wholeheartedly agree!

...I strongly urge you to buy *The Adventures of a Blind and Disabled Award-Winning Author* by Shirley Cheng and you will glean from rare insight.

— *Curtis R. Doll, Jr, SelfGrowth.com Expert on The Beauty of Art, Design and the Spirit*

"Multiple disabilities" should be altered to "multiple abilities!" Shirley Cheng continues to be a powerhouse. Her commitment and motivation to help others and make a difference in this world is overwhelming. Especially after reading and experiencing the challenges she continues to fearlessly face; it is undeniable testimony as to why she is here on this planet with us. I often think of Shirley when I am in a situation and feel overwhelmed beyond my abilities. Her strength and devotion inspires me to do more and to keep the faith, more than ever. The bond between Shirley and her mother is beyond words. If everyone had that kind of support, emotionally and physically, this world would be a much different place.

Thank you, Shirley and Juliet, for your humbled spirit and continuing efforts to change the way you observe things and keep moving forward through the

brick walls. It truly seems there is NOTHING that can hold you back.
— *Trish Lay, Speaker, Leadership/Life Coach*

*The Adventures of a Blind and Disabled Award-Winning Author* will take you into the life and struggles of two people:

A mother who through her love, devotion, loyalty and ability to just push forward all the while disregarding her own illness's and selflessness.

A daughter who is physically disabled, blind, highly intelligent, insightful, talented and who is truly inspired not only by the gift of life but also by the genuine love and respect she has for her mother.

This book reveals a crucial part of Shirley Cheng's life that will be a lesson to all of its readers that a mind inspired by the gift of life can take pain, suffering, misfortune, even busy traffic or bad weather and turn it into something that can be overcome with a single positive thought and the love of life itself. Shirley's continued efforts to create and share her inspirations through her books are commendable. Along her side, her mother continues to struggle with Shirley and overcome obstacles that most of us can not even conceive of. Together they are determined to send a message out to the people that the gift of life, we were so blessed with, should not be treated with disrespect but should be embraced and treasured.

Womensselfesteem.com highly recommends : The Adventures of a Blind and Disabled Award-Winning Author as a definite resource book for anyone that feels that their struggles cannot be overcome. Through this book you will learn how to choose your battles and overcome negative thinking that only drags

you down and depletes you of any positive energy. Do you want to embrace life and learn how to love yourself? Then read Shirley Cheng's thoughts and I promise that you will not be disappointed. Again many thanks to Shirley for her outstanding efforts in sharing her insights with us!
—*Dorothy Lafrinere, Women's Self-Esteem Expert*

    Shirley uses the gift of imagery in such a brilliant manner that you feel as if you are walking through the pages of her life together with her, a part of her and a part of her mother, Juliet.
    Shirley does a truly wonderful job in motivating the reader through her situations, uplifting the reader, inspiring the reader, and causing the reader to look at their own life, their own situations; and making a difference to effect positive changes.
    I laughed, I cried, I was inspired, and I was motivated to action.
—*Leyla Hur, Empowerment Mentor, Radio Host, Speaker, Author, Award-Winning Poet, www.LeylaHur.com*

    If you ever have a bad day, or things in life just aren't working out as you would like, and all this is getting you down, then read Shirley's Adventures and be inspired. Shirley has very honestly and openly described her everyday challenges and writes about her attitudes, thoughts and responses to what she faces repeatedly. There is ample supply of mishaps and difficulties to keep most people complaining for a long time. But Shirley, blind and bound to a wheel chair with limited limb movement, takes it all with a smile and insists on loving life.
    Shirley very honorably describes her mother,

Juliet, and how she helps her in every way... This book will leave you not only admiring Shirley, a blind disabled author, but admiring Juliet, a mother of love and unwavering dedication to her daughter.

Let Shirley inspire you and motivate you to reassessing your life and moving forward with a new determination and goal.

Don't give up. Shirley doesn't!
— *Jim Murdoch, Consultant, Speaker, Life Success Consultants with Bob Proctor and Paul Martinelli*

Shirley Cheng has a unique ability to inspire you to live your full potential. Her wisdom emerged because she embraces all of life, from the thorns surrounding a fragrant rose to the warm kisses of the sun. Experiences most people judge harshly have empowered Shirley to be a shining star on Planet Earth. She reminds all of us to embrace the richness of the human experience and mine the gold that glitters in the darkest tunnels we travel."
— *Doris Helge, Ph.D., Psychologist, Author, Speaker, Radio Host, www.TransformingPainIntoPower.com*

You thought you were at your lowest. You thought you had no hope. You need not walk in Shirley Cheng's shoes just try them on. You will then know what true challenges are. You will know what doing all you can do means. You will know what perpetual optimism is. Dare to take her journey. Dare to ride faith to success.

Shirley Cheng's inspirational mantras are perseverance, persistence, and "limiting limitations." Then, as if forging her own golden path is not enough, she advocates for parental rights and child healthcare, for special needs children in particular, and for all disabled individuals in general. A heart holding that much love is a heart to know. You know quickly where the loving comes from because you meet her mother along the way. Her mother models love, self-sacrifice, and unconditional support.

Walk in Shirley's shoes? That is much too tough. Just try them on for a moment to know your own potential.

*—Parthenia Izzard, Psychologist, CNHP, Radio Host, www.AMTherapies.com*

I feel deeply humbled and grateful to have been asked by Shirley Cheng to review her memoir. You might need to read it twice to fully associate with it, to fully understand and feel the incredible courage, strength, determination, persistence, faith, passion, Shirley has.

The memoir is written in the third person, as if she is talking about someone else, and she makes things seem much easier than I think might have been.

It is a song to life, to love, to God, to the greatness of the human spirit. As for the Chinese proverb: 'A bird does not sing because it has an answer. It sings because it has a song.' Shirley is singing her unique, beautiful, wonderful song for all of us, at the service of humanity.

It is how we respond to what we experience in life that determines our greatness. It is by choosing to find the blessing in it, that we can begin creating a poem, a masterpiece with our life. And that is what Shirley so wonderfully does and teaches us, finding a blessing in the most incredibly painful difficulties.

We can choose to be average or we can choose to be extraordinary. Shirley has clearly chosen to be extraordinary.

Her memoir is also a hymn to the wonderful love between a mother and a daughter. It is also a hymn to what we truly are, spiritual beings, and part of the human family.

—*Piercarla Garusi, Director of PG Coaching, Life Coach, NLP Master Practitioner, www.PGCoaching.co.uk*

# About the Author

Shirley Cheng, born in 1983, a blind and physically disabled award-winning author (with twenty book awards), motivational speaker, self-empowerment expert, poet, and author of nine books and contributor to sixteen, is a miracle survivor with tremendous talents, an exceptionally tenacious spirit, and a colorful personality. She was diagnosed with severe juvenile rheumatoid arthritis at only eleven months old. She spent her early years in constant pain, confined to a wheelchair, and was hospitalized for many years while living between China and America until 1994. Unable to receive any form of education until her health was stabilized, Shirley started attending school at age eleven in a special education class in elementary school. Back then, she knew very little English, and her knowledge on other subjects was non-existent. Miraculously, she mastered grade level in all areas after approximately 180 days of attendance, and she immediately entered a regular sixth grade class in middle school.

Shirley has a voracious appetite for books, reading an average of six hundred pages (three books) daily, and has read over a total of two thousand books. Since sixth grade, she has received 100 on every NYS essay test, and stayed at the top of the class ever since. She was awarded for achieving the highest grade of 97 in Earth science in her eighth grade class. She was the Student of the Year and the Student of the Month, as well as a three-time winner of the National Reflections

Program in visual arts. She has a passion for writing both prose and poetry. One of her short stories, *Mary Miller, the Elusive Lady*, received Honorable Mention and was published by the *Poughkeepsie Journal* in 1997, and her poem, *The Colors of the Rainbow*, earned merit status and was published in *Celebrate! New York Young Poets Speak Out* in 1999.

Shirley was a contributor to her high school newspaper, providing artwork in tenth grade. She received a standing ovation when she delivered a speech as a candidate for student body vice president in ninth grade.

When her eyesight began to deteriorate at the beginning of tenth grade, she had to use two magnifying glasses, holding one on top of the other, on enlarged print to do her work throughout the year, including the artwork she provided for the school newspaper. In classes, she learned only by listening to her teachers, even with chemistry and math, as she was unable to see the blackboard; still she maintained excellent grades.

Unfortunately, Shirley completely lost her vision in April of tenth grade. She then received home-tutoring, and successfully completed all her schoolwork by using cassette tapes and tape recorders. She wrote and balanced long chemistry formulas and equations without vision or Braille (she cannot use Braille because of her severe arthritis). Her high school overall average was 97 (a 3.9 GPA without any advanced placement classes). But Shirley could not accumulate enough credits to receive a high school diploma from her school due to her vision loss. In 2002, she received her high school equivalency diploma. She took the entire GED test, including mathematical calculations, graphs, and an essay, in her head, and received a special recognition award for scoring an exceptionally high 3280. She was a student speaker at the GED graduation ceremony, and received a standing ovation for her speech.

Shirley became an author at age twenty, completing three books within one year. She wrote her books using a screen reader on her computer, typing with her two index fingers at the speed of about sixty words per minute. She successfully completed every self-publishing task, including formatting her manuscripts, on her own.

Shirley wrote her autobiography when she was twenty, and it was first published with the subtitle *A Young Woman's Autobiography of a 20-Year Tale of Trials & Tribulations*, with the ISBN 9781411618602. She inserted, resized, and cropped all the photographs and drawings in this new edition of her autobiography while having her mother Juliet Cheng as her eyes.

In January 2006, Shirley tied for first place in Be the Star You Are! Second Annual Essay Contest founded by New York Times bestselling author, TV/radio personality Cynthia Brian, garnering her a third appearance on Cynthia's live radio show. Shirley's winning entry, titled *The Jewel from Heavenly Father*, is dedicated to her beloved mother. In the following January, Shirley won Honorable Mention in the same contest for her essay, *I Hold the Power*, her personal story of overcoming blindness at the age of seventeen. In January 2008, Shirley was yet again one of the winners in the contest, earning Honorable Mention for her essay, *My Mother: A Fighter, a Victor, a Lover*, which applauds her stellar mother for being a courageous and loving fighter to protect her life at all costs.

Shirley has an immense passion for life and is full of life and vigor. Despite her severe disabilities, Shirley has striven to overcome overwhelming obstacles and she is living the life she loves, while she empowers, inspires, and motivates others to do the same.

Shirley was brought up in a very simple, single-parent, Chinese-speaking family with no influence on education. She pursues her education on her own. She has extraordinary goals with the aspiration of attending college at Harvard University, where she plans to earn doctorates in microbiology, zoology, astronomy, physiology, and pathology, after a successful eye surgery.

Shirley is a true magical gift, a star with endless shine.

# Shirley As an Advocate

Shirley is an advocate of parental rights in children's medical care, and aide/caregiver monitoring and screening for students with special needs and disabled people.

As a parental rights advocate, she wants to help today's loving parents protect and keep custody of their children. "When doctors ask yes or no, parents should have the right to say no," says Shirley, a survivor of two custody battles her mother Juliet Cheng had with doctors.

Shirley's last case made international headlines in 1990; Juliet appeared on *CBS This Morning* with Paula Zahn as she fought to save Shirley's life and prevent her from receiving the harmful treatment recommended by her doctor in Connecticut.

To support Shirley in her good cause, please sign her *Parental Rights in Children's Medical Care: Give Parents the Right to Say No* petition at:

www.petitiononline.com/parentr7/petition.html

Shirley promotes aide advocacy for the disabled because she was mistreated and abused by one-on-one aides when she attended school. "The trouble with uncaring aides actually lies with the authorities," she says. "If they had listened to my complaints and kept a close watch on the aides, I wouldn't have gone through all the suffering."

# Other Books by Shirley

Shirley is also the author of:
- *Daring Quests of Mystics*
ISBN: 978-1-4116-5664-2
- *Embrace Ultra-Ability! Wisdom, Insight & Motivation from the Blind Who Sees Far and Wide*
ISBN: 978-0-6151-5522-7
- *Dance with Your Heart: Tales and Poems That the Heart Tells*
This book is available in Vietnam, published by the Women Publishing House in 2008 and translated into Vietnamese by Nguyen Bich Lan.
ISBN: 978-1-4116-1858-9
- *Waking Spirit: Prose & Poems the Spirit Sings*
(with foreword by New York Times bestselling author Cynthia Brian)
ISBN: 978-0-6151-3680-6 (trade paperback)
978-0-6151-3893-0 (hardback)
- *Parental Rights in Children's Medical Care: Where Is Our Freedom to Say No? A Look at the Injustice of the American Medical System*
ISBN: 978-0-6151-4994-3
- *The Revelation of a Star's Endless Shine: A Young Woman's Autobiography of 20-Year Victories over Victimization*
(foreword by Cynthia Brian)
ISBN: 978-0-6151-5044-4
- *First-Step Guide to Self-Publishing & Promotion*

With highly acclaimed experts, like Dr. Wayne Dyer, Tony Robbins, and Jack Canfield, Shirley co-authored *Wake Up...Live the Life You Love: Finding Life's Passion* and *101 Great Ways to Improve Your Life, Volume 2*.

# Book Awards

*Waking Spirit: Prose & Poems the Spirit Sings* is the recipient of:

• 2009 Silver Recipient of Mom's Choice Awards® in Inspirational/Motivational
• The Avatar Award for Spiritual Excellence in Literature (2008)
• Best book in three categories of Reader Views 2007 Annual Literary Awards: First Place in Poetry Nonfiction, and Second Place in both New Age Nonfiction and Spirituality/Inspiration
• Finalist in the national Indie Excellence 2007 Book Awards
• Honorable Mention in the 2007 New York Book Festival Competition in Poetry
• Honorable Mention in the 2007 DIY Book Festival in Poetry

*Embrace Ultra-Ability! Wisdom, Insight & Motivation from the Blind Who Sees Far and Wide* is the recipient of:

• Reader Views 2008 Literary Awards – Honorable Mention for Body/Mind/Spirit
• Nine Parent to Parent Adding Wisdom Awards, including Adult Health & Well-being, Books – Inspirational/Christian, Gifts for Mom, Gifts for Dad, and Unique Products
• Finalist in the 2008 Next Generation Indie Book Awards in Motivational
• Finalist in the National Best Books 2008 Awards in Philosophy

# Shirley on the WWW

Visit Shirley on the Web at http://www.shirleycheng.com to learn more about her, her books, listen to some of her radio show interviews, E-mail her, and subscribe to her monthly newsletter, *Inspiration from a Blind*, to receive words of inspiration, special news and events information, and exclusive offers for members. Her newsletter issues are archived on her blog, http://blog.shirleycheng.com to which people can subscribe via E-mail or RSS.

Personalized autographed copies of all of Shirley's books are available from her Web site.

Her books are also available through Ingram, from Amazon.com (and their international sites) and BN.com, and also available through brick-and-mortar bookstores (ask your local bookstores and libraries to carry them).

Shirley is available for interviews, speaking engagements, book signings, and inspirational events.

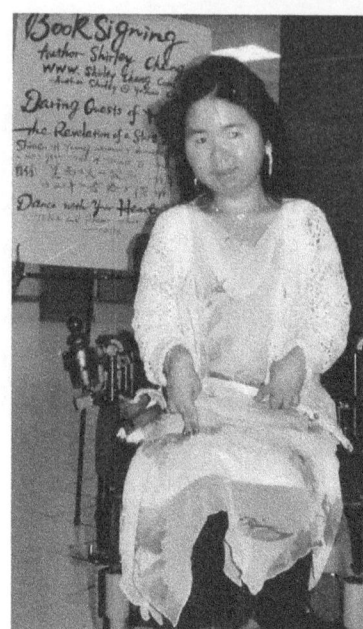

Top left: Shirley Cheng's very first book signing during the Chinese New Year celebration of the Year of the Rooster in February 2005. Top right: Saturday authors luncheon at BookExpo America 2005. Bottom: Shirley in front of Jacob K. Javits Convention Center for BookExpo America 2005 in New York City.

Top left: Shirley's first book signing at Borders Books, Music & Café in August 2006. Top right: Shirley's second signing at Borders in October 2006. Bottom: Shirley holding a signing after giving her inspirational talk during Pine Plains Lions Club zone dinner meeting on April 9, 2007.

Top left: Shirley with Greg S. Reid, "Millionaire Mentor" and writer of *Pass It On*, AlwaysGood.com. Top right: Greg Reid and David Corbin, executive producer of *Pass It On*, DavidCorbin.com. Bottom: Shirley with Jon Dixon, 24, director of *Pass It On*. All photographs here are taken during the film's world premiere in Las Vegas on May 10, 2007 at the Palms Casino Resort inside the Brenden Theatres.

Top left: Bill Bartmann, Billionaire Business Coach, BillionaireU.com.
Top right: David Dean, president of David Dean and Associates, Inc.
Bottom: Charlie "Tremendous" Jones, founder of ExecutiveBooks.com.

Top left: Robin Leach, host of the *Lifestyles of the Rich and Famous* television show. Top right: Shirley after her film shooting session for the *Wake Up...Live the Life You Love* documentary. Bottom: Dr. Michael Beckwith, new thought minister and founder of Agape International Spiritual Center.

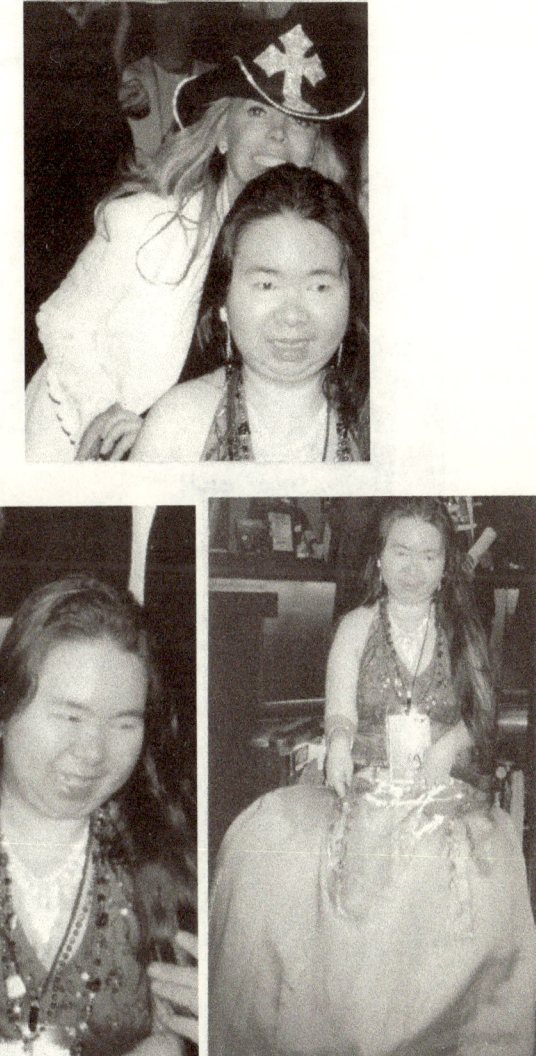

Top: LuAn Mitchell-Halter, corporate executive, author, internationally acclaimed motivational speaker, LuAnMitchell.com. Bottom: Shirley at the *Pass It* On world premiere.

Shirley relaxing in front of the Palms Casino Resort.

Top left: Shirley in front of International Rights Center at BookExpo America 2007. Top right: *Waking Spirit* displayed at New Title Showcase. Bottom: Shirley autographing *Waking Spirit* at table 34.

Top: Robert F. Kennedy Jr. at his autographing table during BookExpo America 2007. Middle: Jack Canfield and Mark Victor Hansen, co-creators of *Chicken Soup for the Soul*. Bottom: Tina Louise, "Ginger Grant" in *Gilligan's Island*.

More of the smiling Shirley at BookExpo America 2007.

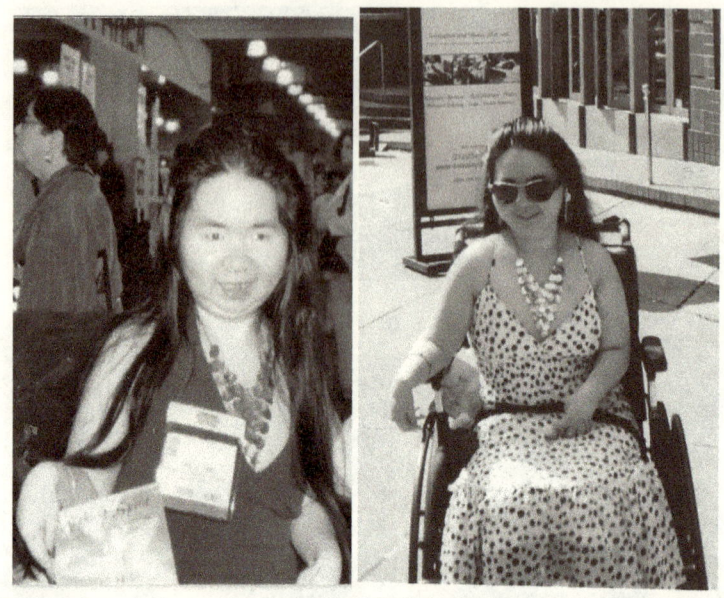

Top: Even more photographs of Shirley enjoying herself at BookExpo America 2007. Bottom: Shirley holding her book signing during the 2007 New York Book Festival in Central Park in New York on June 23, 2007.

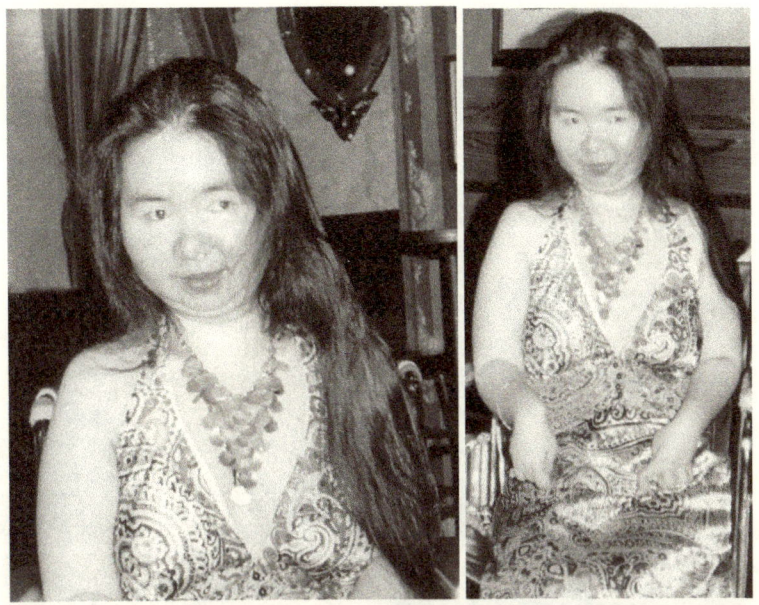

Top: Shirley during the book awards ceremony for the 2007 New York Book Festival where she received Honorable Mention for *Waking Spirit* in the Poetry category. Bottom: Shirley at the entrance of the festival in Central Park.

Shirley posing for a shot during her third book signing at Borders held on June 15, 2007.

www.ingramcontent.com/pod-product-compliance
Lightning Source LLC
Chambersburg PA
CBHW032111090426
**42743CB00007B/316**